Victims
of the Long March

Victims of the Long March

and other stories

John Pollock

WORD BOOKS, Publisher
Waco, Texas
London, England

First Printing—July 1970
Second Printing—October 1970

Library of Congress Catalog Card Number: 79–125270
Printed in the United States of America

Contents

Preface

These sketches first appeared either in *World Vision* or *Crusade* magazines. The men I write about came from North America or from Britain but their influence spread all over the world. Some are household names; three are little remembered today, and I am grateful for the opportunity of recalling them. Most left home to serve—and sometimes to die—in very different climes. But one, James Ramsay, did his finest work for mankind after he had returned home. In some ways he was more influential than any of them, yet his name has virtually perished from the earth.

JOHN POLLOCK

Rose Ash
Devonshire

Acknowledgments

I wish to acknowledge the kindness of editors who gave permission to reprint articles:

To the editor of *Crusade* for the sketches of Ramsay, Edwardes, Radstock, Stanley Smith, and Grenfell.

To the editor of *World Vision* for the sketches of Carey, Judson, Hudson Taylor, Chalmers, Bingham, John and Betty Stam, and Presswood.

1. "All My Friends Are But One"

Outside a tumbledown shed on the edge of a steamy swamp a few miles north of Calcutta sat a dejected Englishman. His name was William Carey. The year was 1794. He was thirty-two years old.

In the shed lay his eldest son, desperately ill of dysentery. Beside the boy lay his mother, not only ill but wandering in mind and bitterly reproaching Carey for having dragged them all from a placid English pastorate across dangerous seas to a land of disappointment and destitution. The three other boys (there was a baby too) could not be allowed out of Carey's sight for fear of dacoits—the thieves and brigands which infested the countryside. Although they would disdain to molest a destitute sahib, since fat Indian moneylenders were easy to find, they could get a good price for a kidnapped white child in native states upcountry.

The Careys had been in India less than two months and everything had gone wrong. As Carey wiped the sweat off his spectacles, picked up his Bible and turned pages already spoiled by mildew, he wondered whether he had mistaken God's call.

It had all begun more than ten years earlier. Carey, then twenty-one and a mere village shoe-maker in the Midlands of England, a man of no account in an aristocratic age but already a fervent Christian, had been reading a borrowed copy of *Captain Cook's Voyages,* an especially topical book because the news of the great explorer's murder by South Sea islanders had only recently reached Europe. Captain Cook was not particularly known as a Christian, yet the book brought the young shoe-maker Christ's orders to serve as His missionary in the South Seas, where none had so much as heard His name.

Missionaries in the 1780s were an almost extinct race. When Carey attempted to enthuse his fellow Baptists with the project, he was rebuffed with the crushing retort: "When God pleases to convert the heathen, he'll do it without consulting you!" Carey became a full-time pastor, and still the Christless millions overseas dominated his prayers, and even turned him into a pamphlet writer.

In 1792 he persuaded his brethren to found the Baptist Missionary Society. They began collecting a little money, in the form of pledges thrust into a snuffbox, and designated Carey their first missionary, to sail to Tahiti as soon as their funds allowed.

"Expect great things from God. Attempt great things for God," Carey had proclaimed. And here he was, little more than a year later, sitting on the edge of an Indian marsh, almost a castaway.

His plan to evangelize the South Seas had been changed through the influence of a surgeon on leave from the British East India Company in Bengal. John Thomas painted a vivid picture of the Hindu civilization of India. His soul was eaten up by compassion for Indian sufferings and zeal for the conversion of Indians to Christ, and he believed the time was ripe.

Carey agreed to go to India, with the Baptist missionary committee's approval, but at the cost of separation from his timid, stay-at-home wife until the mission should be established.

Carey, his eldest son Felix, and John Thomas set sail in 1793, only to be put ashore again. The East India Company was implacably opposed to missions, which might endanger commerical profits by angering the Hindus. A friendly captain had smuggled the three aboard. But creditors pursued Thomas who, though a sincere missionary, was totally irresponsible regarding money.

"All I can say," wrote Carey, watching from a lodging house window the sails of the convoy of East Indiamen disappear over the horizon, "is that however mysterious the leadings of Providence, I have no doubt but that they are superintended by an infinitely wise God."

Ten days later, his lips filled with praise, Carey was

embarking on a Danish ship whose crew cared nothing for the antimissionary growls of the British Company. What is more, Thomas had not only squared his London creditors but Dorothy Carey had rejoined her husband with their whole family, including the new baby.

When the ship reached the mouth of the Ganges, Thomas insisted that they all disembark secretly downstream from Calcutta, partly for fear of more creditors, partly to avoid arrest and expulsion by British officials.

Within two months William Carey, despite the thrill at his first steps in Bengali, of hearing Thomas preach in the crowded Bengal villages, and of all the sights and sounds of India, was on the edge of despair. The sheer weight of Hinduism seemed to crush hopes that a Christian church would arise quickly. Dorothy and Felix fell ill, and Dorothy's mind began to unhinge. Then John Thomas announced that he had misjudged their finances and they were nearly destitute. Carey was reduced to accepting the loan of a native moneylender's garden house in a neighborhood abounding in snakes, tigers, and cutthroat dacoits.

As Carey sat in the steamy heat outside that shed, his wife moaning in the shadows behind, it would have been hard to believe that here was the "father of modern missions" whose translations of the Scriptures would pioneer missionary work in India, whose name, when he died, would be known and honored from Cape Cormorin to the Himalayas.

The would-be missionary to India might have cut

his losses at that moment. The spirit within him was too hot to abandon the ministry—he had heard the call and must follow. But he might have concluded that the door to India was closing, that he had mistaken God's guidance when he had agreed to go to India, and that he had best change back to Tahiti where there was no entrenched Hinduism, where no "Christian" company officials would frustrate his designs.

Carey decided to seek advice from David Brown, a well-known evangelical chaplain to the East India Company's Europeans in Calcutta. He walked through the heat of the city to see Brown, but Brown received him frigidly because of distrust of John Thomas. In later years Brown and Carey would be close friends, but on this January day of 1794 the chaplain sent the ex-cobbler away without even offering him refreshment after his long walk.

"All my friends are but One," thought Carey as he trudged home again, "but He is all sufficient." In his diary he wrote: "Towards evening felt the all-sufficiency of God, and the stability of His promises, which much relieved my mind. As I walked home in the night, was enabled to roll all my cares on Him."

Soon he was allowed to occupy and clear a small area of jungle in another, more healthy district. He intended to support his family by small farming, like the Indians around him, while learning the language and beginning to preach. Then Thomas secured for him the post of manager of an indigo plantation at Malda several hundred miles away, and the whole situation was transformed.

Carey became a well-paid planter with a pleasant home and unrivaled opportunity for getting to know the language, the people, and their customs as he traveled far and wide buying the indigo crop and supervising the processes which turned it into the blue vegetable dye much prized in eighteenth-century Europe. In slack periods he could preach and teach. He had a friendly employer, George Udny, a vigorous Christian who as a magistrate could protect Carey from government attempts to forbid his preaching.

The road ahead was not easy. Carey survived a serious attack of malaria, but his little boy Peter did not. Mrs. Carey fell ill again and began to rail against her husband. For weeks he endured her violence against himself and all he held dear, and because so little was then known about the influence of body upon mind, it was a long time before he realized that her ravings and bitterness were part of her illness. To Carey it seemed that his much-loved Dorothy had become his enemy.

In the midst of these troubles he received a letter from the mission committee in England deploring his being a planter! Had he not, they asked, left England to be a missionary?

A missionary he was. William Carey, planter of Malda in Bengal in the closing years of the eighteenth century, is a sort of patron saint of the many hundreds of men and women today who are not listed as "missionaries," yet are full-time missionaries at heart. They may be in commerce or industry,

United Nations or diplomatic service, or in any of the hundred and one positions open to Western Christians in lands where Christianity is a minority religion, but their vocation and intention is to be witnesses and ambassadors for Christ.

Whereas Carey's employer, George Udny, a devout evangelical, put his secular concerns first (he loved the Bible and encouraged missionaries but never preached to Indians himself), Carey put business concerns last. He lived simply and devoted the bulk of his income to the translation of the Scriptures. "I am indeed poor, and always shall be," he told the home committee, "until the Bible is published in Bengali and Hindustani and the people need no further instruction." His considerable spare time went to translating, or to preaching under the tamarind tree of each teeming village of the district.

The preaching made no impact on the entrenched hold of Hinduism. All around were the miseries imposed by the caste system, yet its iron grip held the hearts of the people to idolatry. As John Thomas, managing a nearby plantation, wrote to the home committee: "Do not send men of compassion here, for you will break their hearts. Do send men *full* of compassion, for many perish with cold, many for lack of bread, and millions for lack of knowledge."

All but two of Carey's handful of converts proved to be frauds or became backsliders. "I am almost grown callous," he wrote in 1799, "and tempted to preach as if their hearts were invulnerable. But this dishonours the grace and power of God." Meanwhile, he and Thomas had completed the translation of the New Testament into Bengali, and Udny had bought them a printing press.

The future again grew obscure. Several bad seasons and a calamitous flood followed by drought and epidemics made Udny determined to abandon his plantations. Carey would be without a home or a job, and four English missionaries with their families were on the outward voyage to join him. He therefore invested all his savings in buying an indigo plantation to form their base.

One of the new missionaries, William Ward, fresh from landing, reached him with the news that they had been offered land and sanctuary. In the tiny Danish enclave of Serampore, British orders of expulsion could not affect them. And Serampore, only fourteen miles upriver from Calcutta, was a strategic center, whereas Malda lay remote.

"Carey has made up his mind to leave all and follow our Saviour to Serampore," wrote Ward. "Indeed, whilst He has opened a door there to us, He has shut all others."

Ward was a printer, his ambition "to *print* among the Gentiles the unsearchable riches of Christ." The other leader of the party, Joshua Marshman, was a self-taught schoolmaster, brilliant but cross-grained, with a wife of inexhaustible good humor. Carey joined them, and for over thirty years the Serampore trio of Carey, Marshman, and Ward was the spearhead of Christian work in India.

How Carey translated the whole Bible into five Indian languages and parts of it into nearly thirty

more; how Ward printed the versions and, as converts came, spread them the length and breadth of
India; how the Marshmans founded schools to support the community and Carey taught in the East
India Company's college in Calcutta, and how they
launched the first mission to Burma which Judson
was to join at their suggestion—all this is part of the
imperishable saga of the growth of the church of
God.

Yet it would have come to naught had the destitute Carey of January 1794 abandoned his Indian
designs and attempted to reach Tahiti. The discour-
aged recruit became the foremost missionary of his
day.

2. Judson's Darkest Hour

The American couple sat down to their meal nervously.

On this June day of 1824 in the Burmese capital of Ava, 400 miles from the sea, Adoniram and Ann Judson, both in their thirties, lived by sufferance of the Burmese king in a little house he had allowed them to build. The home was of teak, which could not keep out the heat of the day, but it was within sight and sound of the royal palace.

The king was contemptuous of their message as Christian missionaries and suspicious of their motive. But richly dressed nobles and even the king himself would condescend to listen to their words occasionally when they visited the royal audience rooms. Yellow-robed Buddhist monks filed past their rough veranda, begging bowls in hand, on the way to the bazaar. Sometimes a priest accepted an invitation to listen to the American teacher's earnest declaration that the Truth could be *known* and that the Way was not a path of merit leading to ultimate Nothingness but a living Person who brought Life.

For twelve years the Judsons had struggled, first in Rangoon, and for the past six months at Ava the capital. Their work had at last begun to show the small beginnings of a Christian church in a Buddhist land. Now all was at hazard again because war had broken out between the Burmese and the British, who had sent an invasion force from India.

The three or four British residents of Ava had already been thrown into prison. This is why the Judsons were nervous as they toyed with their food. The Burmese knew no distinction between the subjects of King George IV and the fellow citizens of President James Monroe.

The Judson dinner had barely begun when a Burmese officer rushed in, accompanied by a knot of men. They were led by a brute whose spotted face and depraved features proclaimed him a jailer—a murderer reprieved on condition that he torture and kill as required.

Despite Ann's protests and her hurried offers of money, Adoniram Judson was thrown to the ground. A cord was deftly wound round his upper arms and chest and tightened until it cut. Then they hurried him away. When Ann sent their Burmese assistant, a convert and true friend, to follow the party and again offer money, the words were barely out of his mouth before the jailer tripped Judson on the pathway and tightened the cords until he could barely breathe.

At the jail he was stripped of most of his clothes, manacled, and placed alongside the other white captives already in the death prison. The tiny compartment was packed with local criminals and crawling with vermin. He was soon joined by his sole American missionary colleague, the bachelor Dr. Price.

June heat and the small size of the windows made misery enough. But at night time an atrocious contraption, a long bamboo pole attached to a pulley, was thrust between the fettered legs of each prisoner and jacked up until the weight of his body and the irons had to rest, all night long, on his shoulders and hands.

In the months that followed, Judson survived only through Ann's indomitable courage. Though expecting a baby she daily spent weary hours walking through Ava to petition officials and nobles. She brought him his only food. She smuggled in his New Testament, and she kept up his courage by brief visits, made at the risk of being arrested herself and sent into slavery.

Years earlier, on his first voyage from America, Judson had been imprisoned in the hold of an English ship after its capture by a French privateer. He had been tempted then to regret his refusal of the assistant minister's post at the largest church in Boston in preference for the hazards of missionary life.

Such temptation had long lost its force. At Ava he

was proving in appalling conditions the accuracy of some gallant words which he had penned in a comfortable New England home when facing the prospect of being the first American preacher in Asia. "O the pleasure which a lively Christian must enjoy in communion with God!" Judson had written. "It is all one whether he is in a city or a desert, among relations or among savage foes, in the heat of the Indies or in the ice of Greenland; his infinite Friend is always at hand. He need not fear want or sickness or pain, for his best Friend does all things well. He need not fear death, though it come in the most shocking form, for death is only a withdrawing of the veil which conceals his dearest Friend."

In those first days in the death house, as his cramped limbs, chilled with loss of circulation, were lowered to the ground in the morning, Judson knew that his dearest Friend was beside him. When the bell began tolling the afternoon hour at which victims would be led out to be beaten or mutilated or crucified, and a ghastly stillness settled on criminals and prisoners of war alike, waiting to know who should be chosen next, Judson proved the peace that passes understanding.

Days lengthened into months. Conditions became slightly better, thanks to Ann's persistence, but a tide of frustration began to mount in Judson's mind.

His beloved converts were scattered. He could no longer go out under the shadow of a golden pagoda to engage passersby in religious conversation. He could do no work on the Burmese dictionary which would enable American reinforcements to learn the

language. Nor could he continue the Burmese translation of the Bible which he knew was an essential
preliminary to the growth of a strong church.

What was worse, his imprisonment, unlike the
Apostle Paul's, did not seem to be furthering the
gospel. It was a mere accident of war. It meant little
to anyone in Ava.

Had Judson been called upon to suffer publicly for
his faith, or to withstand attempted brainwashing
like Geoffrey Bull in China a century and a quarter
later, or even to perform hard manual labor in slavery, he could have borne it. To be condemned to lie
everlastingly doing nothing in a fetid jail day after
day made him depressed and irritable. His faith remained, but his joy was gone.

It returned when the white prisoners were flung
back into the inner prison. Their feet were again
made fast in the stocks, like Paul's and Silas's at
Philippi, and a rumor was strong that they were to
be executed at three in the morning. As the hour
approached Judson grew calm. When he led the
others in prayer his joy at the prospect of the immediate presence of Christ was muted only by sorrow
for his wife.

The rumor was false. Then came a period of fever
which prostrated his body and spirits. Again he was
saved by his wife's intercession. He was allowed to
move into a little bamboo hut—until an awful day
when the weakened Judson and the others were
taken away.

They were to be burned alive as a sacrifice to the
spirits who should then give the Burmese victory over

the English. No announcement was made, however, of their intended fate.

Judson's fetters were removed, together with the shoes and socks with which Ann had kept her husband supplied. The men were roped together two by two and driven like animals down the sandy, flinty road which was baking in the midday sun. On feet which for nearly a year had been allowed no exercise but a brief fettered hobble round the yard and which were now unwontedly bare, blisters grew fast and soon burst. Every step was a torture, and the jailers moved their prisoners fast.

Judson's morale collapsed. As they passed high over a watercourse he contemplated throwing himself and his companion to death. "The parapet is low," he gasped. "There can be no sin in our availing ourselves of the opportunity."

A modern biographer of Judson doubts this story, which he had read in the reminiscences of a fellow prisoner writing thirty years after the event. He considers it "difficult to conceive" that even in temporary desperation such a man as Judson could have contemplated both the sin of suicide and the treachery of leaving his wife alone in a hostile land. But Ann Judson confirms the story herself as it was told to her the next day by her husband: "so great was his agony, he ardently longed to throw himself into the water to be free from misery. But the sin attached to such an act alone prevented."

The Lord's words, "I will keep thee in all thy ways," proved true even when Judson was physically past controlling himself. His Lord was at his side; He was intervening in other ways too. The Bengali servant of one of the prisoners caught up with the column and saw their distress. He pulled off his turban, tore it in two and handed half to his master and half to Judson, who tied it around his feet. The servant supported and half-carried Judson the rest of the way.

The prisoners were by now in such poor shape that the eight-mile journey planned by their jailers had to be broken by a night's rest. A kindhearted Burmese woman risked official wrath to refresh them with fruit. But next day, when they had reached the ruined bamboo dwelling which was to be set on fire as soon as they were chained to stakes inside, the situation had changed.

The high government leader who had plotted their execution had fallen from favor and was summarily executed!

Judson's darkest hour passed. The place of intended immolation became a prison where captivity was less rigorous than at Ava. But Ann, who had followed him into the countryside with their baby daughter, fell seriously ill.

Judson was able, however, to look forward with hope, for the British forces advanced slowly up the Irrawaddy. "Here I have been for ten years preaching the Gospel," he remarked to a fellow prisoner, "to timid listeners who wish to embrace the truth but dare not—beseeching the emperor to grant liberty of conscience to his people, but without success. And now, when all human means seem at an end, God opens the way by leading a Christian nation to subdue the country. It is possible that my life will be spared. If so, with what ardour and gratitude shall I pursue my work. And if not, His will be done: the door will be opened for others who will do the work better."

His life was spared. The door was opened, and in a way he could not have foreseen. The Burmese territory newly annexed by the British (who permitted missionary work unreservedly) contained a race, the Karens, of whom Judson had known nothing at the time of his imprisonment. The Karens were mostly animist, not Buddhist, and listened to the gospel with open ears. The Karen church became the principal base and spearhead of Christianity throughout Burma.

Adoniram Judson bore marks of the iron fetters for the rest of his life. The long imprisonment had marked him in another way too. He could not bear to be idle.

When the American mission grew large, and missionaries developed a tendency to concentrate in the larger centers, Judson pushed out into the wilds. He traveled endlessly among the Karens and Burmese whenever his health permitted. He grudged the time which administrative duties, and even the translation work and scholarship which he loved, forced him to spend at his base.

Wherever he went he preached and baptized. He was in a hurry, as if seeking to recover the years lost in prison. Judson would not wait until a convert had grown old and wise. When any man he met on tour sought baptism, having heard the gospel from a native evangelist, Judson would question him and his neighbors closely. He believed that if the man had been born again the fact would be evident in his transformed life and baptism need not be delayed. Judson was seldom deceived, and the Karen church grew fast.

Before the prison years, evangelization had depended almost entirely on his own labors. When Judson's feet were bound in the stocks, the Word of God had seemed shackled. He sought therefore to extend himself by urging his converts to go out two by two through the jungle paths to distant villages. He was among the first missionaries to teach that a church must be self-propagating. Thus the Karen church grew and became strong. Its members were outward looking, willing to suffer hardship, danger, and long absences from home to enable others to know Christ as the One who delivers from fear and despair.

Judson's twenty months of stench and frustration in Ava's jails had not been futile after all.

tain, who was concerned at the financial loss which plague would cause yet cared nothing for the slaves as human beings; and the glee with which the crew showed off the brutal instruments used to coerce or punish. Ramsay felt sick.

He gave such treatment as he could, and left medicine and instructions. Meanwhile the *Arundel* had taken the slaver in tow, and Ramsay returned to his ship. All that morning his thoughts and eyes reverted to the ship they were towing. At noon the hawser broke. An hour later the two ships parted, and the *Arundel* increased sail and was away. By evening the slaver with her cargo of misery had dropped below the horizon, but not out of Ramsay's mind. He vowed that he would henceforth do his utmost for slaves. What, however, could be done by an insignificant naval surgeon? God knew the answer.

Three years later Ramsay was a West Indian parson—and a slave-owner himself. A serious fall on board ship and a badly broken leg had incapacitated him for sea service. He had decided to take Holy Orders and dedicate his life to the slaves, and in 1762 he had been appointed through Captain Middleton to a living in the little West Indian island of St. Kitt's. He married a settler's daughter and bought ten slaves, without which he could not have run his household, resolving to prove to his fellow owners "how much might be done by one in earnest."

Thus, on any evening in the following years, a passer-by might have noticed an unwonted sight on the rectory verandah. The ten slaves, their wives and children, stood humbly in a group before their master, lisping the Lord's Prayer at his dictation and listening open-mouthed to the story of Jesus. No slaves could expect to be happier. Work was light, punishment was not severe, and they had every medical attention. But though the slaves were soon "plump, healthy and full of spirits," Ramsay found at the end of ten years that he "possessed not a single slave on whom he could place confidence." Not one had become a true Christian, and two had been sold off as intractable.

Nor were his efforts among the slave-owners successful. When, as surgeon to the plantations, Ramsay was called to attend recalcitrant slaves who had been flogged to an inch of death, or branded on chest, face, or arms, he was cursed for interference if he attempted to protest. On asking that slaves should be allowed Sunday rest and religious instruction he was roundly told not to encourage idleness. His efforts to gather together the slaves of his parish for public instruction received "bitter censure." At last there came an awful Sunday morning in the parish church when Ramsay was bold enough to insert in the Bidding Prayer a petition for the conversion of the blacks. Immediately there was a rustle in the pews. Two or three planter couples stalked out.

When it became known that the rector actually had visions of the eventual abolition of slavery, St. Kitt's was enraged. The Churchwardens presented Ramsay with a formal protest against "neglect of his parish." He was deprived of his magistracy, attacked in the island's newspaper, and ostracized. Depressed and aged by the violence of the storm, Ramsay was tempted to doubt and despair. God seemed to have set him against a brick wall.

War broke out again, and Ramsay took a naval chaplaincy; St. Kitt's was delighted. He never saw the island again, and by the end of 1781 he was rector of Captain Middleton's little village in the English countryside of Kent.

The cry of the slaves haunted him. Often in the evenings he would sit in the drawing room of the great house, Barham Court, and tell Lady Middleton and the two spinster friends who lived with her, "Mrs" Bouverie and "Mrs" Twysden, of the horrors of slavery. Ramsay was only forty-eight, but his grey hair, sad eyes, and lean face seemed to reflect the sufferings he had seen in the Negroes. The agony of the "Middle Passage," the indignities of the slave warehouse, and the brutal manner in which human beings were bought and sold like cattle; the crowded sickhouses with their nauseating stench and filth, the overlong hours of labor under a tropical sun and the overseer's whip—all this he told in graphic terms, arousing in the ladies' hearts a determination to protest.

Lady Middleton was the most outspoken of the three, and one day she sat down at her escritoire and wrote him a long letter, begging him to set before the world the temporal and eternal needs of the slaves. The letter was handed to Ramsay the next morning by Nestor, the Negro who had served him since shortly before the return to England, whose "neat

35

dress, chaste sober life and inoffensive manner subdued the prejudices his colour raised," and who "from his humble station fixed his faith in Christ and looked up to heaven for happiness."

The letter threw Ramsay into a turmoil. He longed to act on Lady Middleton's advice, but feared to face again the "censure and abuse" it was sure to bring. But, as Ramsay said later, "her importunities were great respecting it." Behind her he could sense the quiet insistence of Christ, who for Ramsay's sake, and for the slaves and all men had "endured the cross, despising the shame."

The book was begun. Then the folly of attacking "the interest and majesty of plantership" once more overcame him, and he laid the manuscript aside. The Bishop of London, who had a country house nearby and was a warm friend to the slaves, urged him to resume, and at long last, on a summer's day of 1784, James Ramsay sat anxiously in his study at Teston Rectory, knowing that his mild and constructive book was in the hands of the public.

The storm burst. "Fie! Fie! Mr. Ramsay," cried the West Indian press, "you ought to blush indeed! Ill-natured, wicked, mistaken—deserves punishment for such a libel." "Gross misrepresentations . . . absurdest prejudices," claimed the planters' representatives in London. But if he was abused, to his acute pain and distress, Ramsay was encouraged also, by the many hitherto scattered who made themselves known to him as friends of the cause.

Men whose names were to resound across the world as abolitionists found their way to Teston, and the rectory guest-room was in continual use—Granville Sharp, young Thomas Clarkson fresh from Cambridge, Ignatius Latrobe, the gentle and musical Moravian. Each had written or spoken against slavery but had never met the others.

The months dragged by. Ramsay no longer felt useless and frustrated, a hostage to faith, although the slaves continued to live in misery and die in spiritual darkness, and every trade wind brought fresh cargoes of human cattle. The next step, however, was near.

Ignatius Latrobe stayed at the rectory. Ramsay took him one morning through the park gates, past the new orangery and up to Barham Court for breakfast. In the manner of the day the party sat round the table long after the plates were cleared and the last cups of coffee drunk. As was inevitable, the conversation turned to slavery. Lady Middleton was waxing indignant—"Some very animated expressions of her feelings," recalled Latrobe, "on considering the national guilt attached to the continuation of such a traffic." Ramsay listened, grateful that his seed had borne such fruit in her mind.

She turned to her husband, then in Parliament, and said, "Indeed, Sir Charles, I think you ought to bring the subject before the House." Her words startled the whole table. Occasional resolutions against the Slave Trade had received short shift. To marshal support until the Commons appointed an inquiry would be a long and thankless task needing eloquence, yet Middleton had only made four of the briefest of speeches and was busy with his work at the Admiralty—he was the man whose faithfulness and persistence prepared the Royal Navy for Trafalgar.

Ramsay waited, praying in his heart, for Middleton's answer. "You are right, my lady," Ramsay heard him say at last, "but the cause would be in bad hands if committed to me. But I will strenuously support any able member who will undertake it." They fell to discussing possible leaders. Mrs. Bouverie suggested one, Ramsay another, and timid Mrs. Twysden ventured on a third, but all lacked the ability required. And then someone—they could never remember who—suggested a young *beau,* the Member for Hull, who had been so splendidly converted a short while before: William Wilberforce.

Sir Charles promised to write to him. A few days later Ramsay and Latrobe were again at Barham Court and heard Lady Middleton read Wilberforce's reply. Though some months were to pass before a firm decision, James Ramsay's cause had found a leader.

In the hectic times that followed, Teston was the center of the abolition campaign, and Ramsay its unofficial secretary. The appointment of a Privy Council Committee of Enquiry through Wilberforce's friendship with Pitt enormously increased his work, and Mrs. Ramsay watched anxiously as he pushed his frail body to its utmost. But their hearts were gay as the spring of 1789 drew on, for victory seemed in sight.

"Mr. Wilberforce and whole junta of Abolitionists are locked up at Teston," wrote Hannah More in the early spring of 1789, "they are up *slaving* till two o'clock every morning." The path between the rectory and Barham Court was in constant use, while as the days grew warmer the discussions continued in the garden, under the cedar tree which stands today. And from time to time they would gather for prayer in the tiny parish church beyond the rectory wall.

On May 12, 1789, Wilberforce introduced his Bill for the Abolition of the Slave Trade, and Ramsay was in the happy little party which waited in the Wilberforce house in Palace Yard, their hearts high with praise to God. He did not stay for the debate and was back in Teston when it began to bog down as the slave-owners' friends attacked the Bill with every weapon they could muster. Ramsay's old fears returned. The victory for which he had prayed seemed to recede, until on May 21st a blow fell which he was unable to parry: a Member lampooned him in one of the bitterest speeches of the session, raking up every slander and cruel jibe that had been flung in St. Kitt's. Middleton sprang to his rescue, but when Ramsay read the speech at Teston his nerve broke. Depression was made worse by weariness of body.

The Middletons pressed him to go for a holiday. After delays and hesitations he set out, but at the Middletons' London house, the first stage of his journey, he died.

Forty-three years later, when slavery was abolished throughout the British Empire and the dying Wilberforce received the great praise which was his due, few remembered Ramsay, who in the course of his ordinary duties had heard God's call to attack a great injustice which everyone took for granted.

Fewer today are aware of him, or of the epitaph still to be seen on the wall of Teston Church near Maidstone in Kent: "His Christian love and generous exertions no disappointments could exhaust, calumny slacken or persecution abate."

4. Young Man with a Pigtail

*O*ld *carpenter Wang wan-*
dered down the street toward the river, the mighty
Yangtze, so broad that the farther shore looked like
a mere smudge on the horizon.

All around were the familiar sights and sounds of
a small Chinese town of the eighteen-fifties: loose-
trousered peasants carrying their baskets on long
bamboo poles across their shoulders, vendors shout-
ing their wares, women hobbling in tightly bound
little feet; a teacher in the robe of his class trod
delicately to avoid the offal; scavenger dogs snarled
and fought. Wang knew no other world. He had
heard of Outer Barbarians beyond the Middle Kingdom, and pitied them that they could never taste
civilization, though he had been told that a few of

the more adventurous traded with the Celestial Empire.

His eye caught sight of a knot of excited townsfolk, and as he drew near he saw an extraordinary sight —a "foreign devil." No wonder the crowd was amused: the young man had sandy hair and large grey-blue eyes, a most odd combination for a human being. And even odder were his clothes—black trousers like a coolie's only narrower, black coat complete with pleats and buttons back and front reaching to his knees, leather boots. And no pigtail.

The foreign devil answered questions patiently and began to preach . . . about one Jesus who came into the world and died on a cross, like the poor criminals, Wang supposed, whom sometimes you saw suffer the "death of a thousand pieces." Wang caught snatches. But he could not pay close attention. He was absorbed in study of the foreign devil's amazing clothes, and edged closer to get a better view until almost next to the man, who evidently spotted this rapt interest and directed his talk right at him.

The foreigner paused.

Wang spoke up. "Yes, yes," he said, "What you say is doubtless very true. But, honorable Foreign Teacher, may I ask you a question?"

The young foreigner looked delighted.

"Foreign Teacher, I have been pondering all the while you have been preaching. But the subject is no clearer to my mind. The honorable garment you are wearing has upon one edge of it a number of circular objects that might do duty as buttons, and on the opposite edge, certain slits in the material probably intended for buttonholes?"

The Foreign Teacher seemed disappointed. "Yes, that is so," he murmured.

"The purpose of that strange device I can understand," Wang continued. "It must be to attach the honorable garment in cold or windy weather. But, Foreign Teacher, this is what I cannot understand. What can be the meaning of those buttons in *the middle of the honorable back?*"

"Why, yes," chorused Wang's neighbors, "in the middle of the back!"

The poor deflated preacher (who had no idea why a Victorian frock coat always had three buttons in the small of the back) soon wandered sadly away, for after Wang's question he was quite unable to draw the crowd back to the great subject of the Good News he risked his life to bring to inland China, where no foreigner might lawfully go.

James Hudson Taylor, the Foreign Teacher as Wang had called him, was only twenty-three. He came from Yorkshire, England, and had been in China two years. He was small and of sickly physique, which today probably would never have passed the doctors. He was impulsive, warm-hearted and merry, though with a streak of introspective melancholy. His consuming passion was to win Chinese to Christ. He felt thoroughly impatient with the little band of missionaries then in China, who clung to the coast attempting to reproduce for the Chinese the church life and church buildings of America and England.

Hudson Taylor had gone inland. Yet his attempts were failing because he was a foreigner . . . "In the middle of the honorable back"—the words flung themselves at him, summing up the absurdity of wearing western dress in the China of those days, where everything foreign was utterly despised.

To put on Chinese dress, pigtail and all, would scandalize brother missionaries, infuriate Western merchants who would consider that he had betrayed the British Empire by demeaning himself in the eyes of the natives. Hudson Taylor, however, had already seen what would not be generally accepted by missionaries for another two generations. As he wrote some years later: "Why should a foreign aspect be given to Christianity? We wish to see churches of such believers presided over by pastors and officers of their own countrymen, worshipping God in their own tongue, in edifices of a thoroughly native style."

A century ago such words were revolutionary. Their spirit remains pertinent, for if differences of dress are no longer a wall between Westerners and Orientals, other barriers remain, or are thrown up. Western superiority, Western confidence that we know best, still bedevils many missionary situations, and Hudson Taylor points to the way out—the way of identification. And to the cost: when he adopted Chinese dress, pigtail and all, he lost the respect of his Western contemporaries. But he won the love of the Chinese, could travel widely, be heard quietly, free from urchins who jeered "Foreign Devil!" and earnest inquirers who ruined open-air sermons by awkward questions about buttons.

Furthermore, Hudson Taylor is proof that youth is no bar to being God's recipient of new insights. He is a lasting example of the lead that young men (or women) may sometimes give the church of Christ if they are walking close to Him and will let Him grant them imagination, courage, and persistence, even when, like Hudson Taylor, they are obscure in name and background, without wealth or influence or particularly good health.

The long life of Hudson Taylor, founder of the China Inland Mission (now the Overseas Missionary Fellowship) and one of the greatest of all missionaries, teaches many other lessons, such as the Principle of Faith immortalized by his words, "Depend upon it, God's work done in God's way will never lack for supplies." And the realization that the way to get men and means for the mission field is to deepen the churches until, imbued with the Holy Spirit, their priorities come right and they put the spread of the gospel before the solace of themselves.

Before he could teach such lessons or find his lifework, the opening of all inland China to the Word of God, the young Hudson Taylor had to learn that courage, initiative, and passion for souls are not enough.

In 1856, about a year after the incident of the Buttons-in-the-Honorable-Back, Hudson Taylor in his pigtail, rock-crystal spectacles, and teacher's robe, returned to Shanghai from Swatow, a notoriously wicked tropical port nearly a thousand miles to the south, where with an elderly Scottish missionary he had labored happily, if haphazardly and without apparent effect, for five months. Unable to secure a preaching hall Taylor, who was a physician though not yet qualified, knew what he would do—sail back up the coast to Shanghai, collect medicines and his surgical instruments, and return to labor on in Swatow.

He reached Shanghai to find the building where he had left his entire stock of medical supplies burned to cinders. Except for a few instruments all was gone. "My disappointment and trial were very great," he wrote. Vexed and puzzled he determined to go down the network of canals to Ningpo, the next Treaty Port, where he might buy some replacements from a missionary friend; afterwards he would sail to Swatow.

In the intense summer heat he traveled at a leisurely pace preaching and distributing tracts, until the low level of the Grand Canal made further progress by boat impossible. Taylor set out before sunrise through a district disturbed by civil strife, intending to reach a seaport whence he could take a junk to Ningpo.

Everything went wrong. Leaving his servant (whom he had only recently engaged) to bring on the baggage coolies, Taylor hobbled off in his tight Chinese shoes. At the first stage he had a tedious wait in a tea-shop before the coolies straggled in exhausted. They were opium smokers. He dismissed them, and made the servant engage others, and stupidly walked ahead.

He never saw servant, coolies, or baggage again. At the second stage he waited hours. "I felt somewhat annoyed and but that my feet were blistered and the afternoon very hot, I should have gone back to meet them and urge them on." At dusk there was no sign except a rumor that they had passed through towards the sea. Taylor spent a miserable flea-ridden night in the public dormitory of a tumbledown inn, and awoke feeling sick. Next day he pushed towards the coast, and though at a half-way house during a short shower of rain he managed to preach a little, he reached the seaport upset and unhappy.

Inquiries were fruitless. He was questioned by the police who saw that he was a foreigner. At dusk he was refused by two inns because the police were shadowing him, and turned out of another which at first had accepted him. Still searching for a bed he was led around, desperately tired and sore, by a young man who pretended to be friendly but deserted him at one in the morning, so that he had to sleep in the open on the rough steps of a temple where he was in danger of murder by three thieves. He kept himself awake by singing hymns and repeating portions of Scripture and praying aloud in English until the ruffians disappeared in disgust. At last he slept.

He was awakened rudely at sunrise by the young man, who demanded payment for his time the previous night. This was the last straw. When the fellow laid hands on him Hudson Taylor lost his temper. He grasped the man's arm and shouted at him to shut up.

Everything, everyone was against Hudson. The baggage containing almost all he possessed had been stolen by his faithless servant. Any hope of getting to Ningpo was lost and somehow, almost penniless, entirely friendless, he must return to Shanghai. He dragged blistered feet eight miles of physical misery, in anger and spiritual rebellion, to the place where he had spent the night in the inn. He managed to bathe his feet, eat, and have four hours refreshing sleep in the early afternoon.

He walked on, a little less upset, still puzzled. Surely God had intended him to reach Ningpo; it was the obvious course. Why this abandonment? Had he not surrendered home and comfort and safety on God's behalf?

Before the first milestone it dawned on him that he had *denied his Lord*.

Tension suddenly slacked. Anger and pain dissolved in repentance as the truth broke through that he had not asked for guidance or provision before sleeping in the temple steps. He had lost his temper, thoroughly un-Christlike. He had fussed, worried, forgotten the souls around. He had resented disasters, had expected God to order his affairs as he, Hudson, thought best. "I came as a sinner and pleaded the blood of Jesus, realizing that I was accepted in Him, pardoned, cleansed, sanctified—and oh the love of Jesus, how great I felt it to be."

Hudson Taylor's troubles were not over, but the glorious sense of the love of his Lord swallowed up the miles.

The initiative, the control had passed to Christ—and that was what God had been waiting for.

When at length Taylor reached Shanghai, he received a letter posted in England months earlier which contained a check for exactly the amount of his loss. And before long he discovered that had he got through to Ningpo when he had intended he would have reached Swatow in time to have been imprisoned, perhaps executed.

Words Hudson Taylor wrote at this time come shining through the mist of more than a hundred years. "At home you can never know what it is to be alone—absolutely alone, amidst thousands, without one friend, one companion, everyone looking on you with curiosity, with contempt, with suspicion or with dislike. Thus to learn what it is to be despised and rejected of man—of those you wish to benefit, your motives not understood but suspected—thus to learn what it is to have nowhere to lay your head; and then to have the love of Jesus applied to your heart by the Holy Spirit—His holy, self-denying love, which led Him to suffer this and more than this—for *me this is precious,* this is *worth* coming for."

5. He Tamed the Tribes

*E*arly *in 1847 a young sub-*altern of Bengal Infantry set out on a task to quell the stoutest. Lieutenant Herbert Edwardes had been ordered from Peshawar, the dust-ridden frontier town of the Punjab at the foot of the wild Khyber Pass, to bring peace and government to the Bannu Valley.

Bannu was a paradise of nature, but its people were lawless, "robbers and murderers from their cradles." They butchered one another and refused to pay taxes to their overlords, the Sikhs, whom the British had lately conquered. As Edwardes said, they "wear arms as we wear clothes, and use them as we use knives and forks," while the Sikh soldiers with him would be looking for nothing but loot.

Edwardes, a vivacious young man with laughing

eyes who could as easily turn from soldiering to writing essays and verses, and who had a remarkable capacity for friendship, was not afraid. He had fought in the recent war with distinction, but courage of a different kind was needed now. His fearlessness sprang from his faith. He believed that it was God who was sending him to heal a tortured land. And he knew that his Savior was beside him as the column toiled upwards beneath forbidding rocks and over turbulent streams, with the hot Indian sun above.

When Edwardes reached the Valley, some of the Bannus fled to the hills, others stayed in sullen fear. Soon they were astonished by this lone Englishman whose strange power belied his youthful face. They saw looting suppressed by instant punishment. When, suspicious and diffident, they brought complaints and arguments, Edwardes heard them with patience, good humor, and kindness. When they tried to deceive him, he knew instinctively and would punish them as he punished the Sikhs. Warring chiefs were soon sitting together beside him, four hundred forts were destroyed at his word, even the taxes were paid. "In my little sphere," he wrote, "I gave my whole soul for the establishment of that vast and priceless blessing, peace." And early each morning, in the quiet of his tent, Edwardes would lay all his problems, dangers, and hopes before his Lord.

The pacification of Bannu was the first of many achievements which brought Edwardes resounding fame—crushing rebellion at Multan, bringing peace and prosperity to the intractable tribes of Jalandhar, and negotiating in the face of official opposition and disbelief a treaty of alliance with the powerful Amir of Afghanistan. But good administration was not enough. Edwardes' greatest desire was to see the fanatical Muslims of the hills and the Hindus of the plains united at the foot of the Cross. As agent of the government he was forbidden to preach, but when a fellow officer, Colonel Martin, approached him as Commissioner of Peshawar for leave to found a mission, Edwardes gave wholehearted support, and in 1855 was able to introduce the first two missionaries of the Border Mission and see the first native Christian baptized.

Edwardes was one of that remarkable band of unashamed Christians who transformed the tyrannized, blood-drenched Sikh kingdom into the prosperous and contented British Punjab. The gay Henry Lawrence, "father" and master of them all, who was killed in the siege of Lucknow; his wife Honoria, who rode with them, worked, prayed, and endured with them; his brother John, afterwards Viceroy, dour and severe but earnest in his faith; young Nicholson, who died a hero's death at Delhi; Thomason, Hodson, Abbott—the basis of their life was faith in Christ. "This morning he read a chapter of the Bible to George and me," wrote Edwardes of Henry Lawrence at Lucknow during a visit a bare month before the Mutiny, "and then he prayed with great earnestness . . . The whole prayer was for peace and forbearance and good-will and the help of Christ Himself in our whole lives."

By their Christian characters such administrators

did much to prove to Eastern races the love and power of Christ. They would have done more. "The greatest and oldest and saddest of India's wants," said Edwardes, "is religious truth, a revelation of the real nature of the God whom for ages she has been ignorantly worshipping." Edwardes and his friends recognized that the government itself could not attempt to convert, but they believed the accepted policy of absolute religious neutrality to be harmful. Had the Bible been taught in the native schools, false views of Christianity would not have spread, the Mutiny might never have occurred, and India would steadily have yielded to Christ. "An open Bible," pleaded Edwardes, "put it in your schools, stand avowedly as a Christian government." Only then would India be truly fitted for freedom, "leavened with Christianity."

When the storm came in '57, the Punjab stood firm. The Afghans abided by Edwardes' treaty and took no advantage of British troubles. At Peshawar Edwardes and Nicholson boldly disarmed the mutinous regiments; "if Peshawar goes," a loyal Sikh sirdar had said, "the whole Punjab will be rolled up in rebellion." And had the Punjab revolted, all Bengal might have fallen.

Yet it is not the statesmanship of Sir Herbert Edwardes that is relevant today so much as his witness to a layman's influence for Christ in the ordinary course of his calling. "I never knew anyone so bold in confessing Christ as Edwardes was," said a brother officer on the Frontier. "Many of us felt as he did but we had not the courage to avow it." "This great country India," Edwardes would say, "has been put into our hands that we may give it light." Edwardes' words are still a challenge: "other dependent races in other parts of the world are equally in heathen darkness. If we are looking for the coming of our Lord again upon the earth, we surely should bestir ourselves to gather in as much of His inheritance as we can while time is left."

Edwardes was barely forty-nine when he died, on sick leave in Scotland in 1869. "Jesus only . . . Triumphant Jesus," were his last words; "I am quite happy. I trust entirely to Jesus and I couldn't do more if I lived a thousand years!"

The news was telegraphed to India and carried into the hills. An old, bent Muslim heard it and found his way to a missionary. "I lived with Sir Herbert all the years he has been in India," said the old servant, "and I followed him everywhere. My sahib was *such* a good man. He can't have made a mistake in his religion. Will you teach me his religion? for I should like to believe what he believed."

6. "Lord Apostol"

Colonel Paschkov, wealthy darling of St. Petersburg society, lolled back in his sumptuous, elegant carriage as it took him swiftly from the palace of his Sovereign and personal friend, Alexander II, Tsar of all the Russias, to a soiree given by a Grand Duchess, a member of the Imperial Family. He thought with satisfaction of his popularity, of his vast estates in the Urals, where his thousands of toiling peasants provided him the wherewithal to live in the extravagant luxury to which he had been bred.

At the Grand Duchess's, gilded doors swung noiselessly open and footmen bowed as the Colonel, resplendent in his Guards' uniform, walked with nonchalant hauteur towards the red-carpeted staircase.

The major-domo at the entrance to the great ball-
room did not announce him, but respectfully murmured that the guests of her Imperial Highness were
already seated. Surprised, Paschkov looked across
the long room with its Chinese silks and priceless
works of art and saw a circle of fashionably dressed
men and women, most of whom he knew, sitting
listening to a plainly dressed gentleman with an
English face who stood close to the vast fireplace,
talking quietly but earnestly in French, the normal
language of the Russian nobility.

Intrigued, Paschkov took a seat and listened. "This
same Jesus," the Englishman was saying, and the
words seemed strangely out of place in such sur-
roundings, "who sought the fallen woman of Sa-
maria, and Saul of Tarsus, is alive still, the Son of
Man, 'who came to seek and to save that which was
lost.' " Soon the theme changed, and without raising
his voice the speaker was castigating the selfish luxury and idleness of his hearers; and his bluntness
shook Colonel Paschkov, who had never realized before how empty and self-centered life had been. Then
the theme changed again, passing from the certainty
of judgment to the wonder of a Savior who died on
the cross. Despite himself, Paschkov was stirred to
the depths. This was so different from the contemporary Orthodox Church, with the "insipidity of its
traditional bakemeats served by the official clergy in
their heavy plates of gold"; it was personal and alive.

As the address closed Paschkov urgently asked his
neighbor, a Prince (the highest rank below the Imperial Family) who the man was. "An English milord,"

the Prince whispered back, "Lord Radstock. The Grand Duchess met him in Paris. She's been a different woman since." That night, kneeling beside Lord Radstock, a Bible open between them, Paschkov gave his life to Christ . . . .

It was a few months later in this season of 1873–4. The Minister of the Interior, the clever and cynical Count Brobrinsky, was annoyed. His wife had got herself mixed up with this ridiculous "drawing-room revival" and had just told him that the cause of all the trouble was coming to dinner. Brobrinsky, who had been reading the latest novel, a brilliant skit called *Lord Apostol* which neatly took off the English milord and his absurd converts, had no wish to meet him, but to be absent would be insulting. At dinner, as course after course was handed round on gold plate, Brobrinsky listened with half-amused tolerance as Radstock, who appeared to have no idea as to what subjects were taboo at table, discoursed on the Epistle to the Romans. The Count was frankly agnostic, though to satisfy a vow he had once made when he had believed himself dying he used to say a prayer each day to the Unknown God.

Brobrinsky was certain he could refute all Radstock's statements—the fact of Christ, His resurrection and the possibility of personal faith. When the dessert came, he excused himself, went into his study, and wrote a long refutation which so pleased him that he sent it to be printed. But the eyes and the quiet conviction of the "Lord Apostol," and his sense of the reality of Christ, haunted Brobrinsky.

When the manuscript returned and he began to read it, something snapped. As with a flash of light, "I found that Jesus was the key, the beginning and the end of all." He fell on his knees, Cabinet Minister though he was; the Unknown God had revealed Himself . . . .

Young Princess Catherine Galitzine one day that same year went round in her sleigh through the winter streets to see a newly married friend, Princess Lieven. Both were devout, their emotional natures drinking in the ritual and stately ceremonial of the Greek Orthodox Church. The quarterly reception of the Communion had just taken place, and religion filled Princess Catherine's heart. Her one distress was that the glorious feelings would so soon evaporate, and she must labor on until grace could once more be received at the next Communion.

As she ran lightly up the wide staircase of the palace, the boudoir door opened and Princess Lieven, in her rich brocaded day dress, hurried down to meet her. Lord Radstock had come to call. The two girls began to tell him breathlessly of the happiness the Communion had brought.

"Would you like to possess it for ever?" he asked.

"Impossible," they said.

"And thereupon," Princess Catherine recalled in her old age, "commenced the Message of Grace offered us, without the least pressure on our most precious feelings. Henceforth all the addresses, the meetings to which we hastened, became as seeds which the Lord brought to life. At length, one day, in the American Chapel, after a most blessed address when the never-to-be-forgotten hymn, 'I do believe, I will believe that Jesus died *for me*' was sung, I remained for a special conversation—and there we were both on our knees before *my own Savior for ever."* . . .

"Who is Lord Radstock?"—the question was heard continually as he visited and revisited St. Petersburg and Moscow. Wealthy guardsmen such as Paschkov threw open their palaces to reach the poorest with the gospel; Brobrinsky set himself to win the great novelist Tolstoy; counts and princes began to treat their peasants as human beings; and great estates became centers of evangelism.

He had been born in 1833, the son of an Admiral who after his retirement had spent many years of Christian work. By the time he inherited the title in 1857 Lord Radstock had become a Christian through the influence of his mother, and in intervals of soldiering with the newly raised Volunteers, and absorption in music and literature, he and his young wife, a famous beauty, had given select Bible Readings in their house in Bryanston Square.

Revival was moving across England in 1859, and for Lord and Lady Radstock it brought a call to deliberate service among their own class. Screwing up his courage, Radstock began to give out tracts, with a polite lifting of his top hat, at the daily parades of wealth and fashion in Hyde Park, when all the world sauntered or rode or sat in gleaming carriages, to exchange the gossip of Mayfair and Belgravia. Radstock's tracts, and his invitations to gospel addresses in the Bryanston Square drawing room and his Hampshire seat disgusted his rich titled contemporaries, secure in their regular churchgoing and the respectability which too often camouflaged a carefully hidden immorality.

Despite a life transformed here and there it seemed, as so often before, that a man could not reach his own sort, and Radstock turned to the poor who were never far from the streets of fashion in Victorian England. He built them mission halls and refuge centers, and could often be found preaching in the East End of London. As the revival spread in the sixties he became an evangelist who filled halls in watering places and inland towns, moving from mission to mission. In 1867 he was invited to a conference of the Evangelical Alliance in Holland, and the severe, sober, rigidly correct Dutch Calvinist nobility discovered that God could use him to bring them warm personal faith.

After Holland Lord Radstock went to Paris, brilliant capital of the Second Empire, where the ladies of the court in their huge crinolines danced and flirted oblivious of coming disaster. All the aristocracy of Europe flocked to Paris, and it was among visiting Russians that Radstock found himself most used. His energy was inexhaustible, and he was forever thinking up fresh schemes of evangelization. His impetuousness and bluntness would attract some and alienate others, but those who knew him well were shamed by an unwavering devotion and constancy, by his prayer life, and by his tact in personal dealings, abrupt though he might be in his addresses.

Above all Lord Radstock had that indefinable touch of a man who has learned the secret of steady abiding in Christ. He seemed never to lose contact, however busy the day, and thus had an uncanny knack of being in the right place at the right time, even when a minute or two made all the difference. What others might call coincidences were continually occurring, and it was in this way that he met the Grand Duchess, who had previously refused categorically to be introduced to such a man. But she happened to arrive, uninvited, to spend an evening with a Princess; by a series of "chances" Lord Radstock was unexpectedly with the Princess when the Grand Duchess was announced. And after her conversion she invited him to Russia.

The Russian Revival went from strength to strength—Lord Radstock, whose Russian was not fluent enough for preaching, working in the drawing rooms and his converts going out among the poorer classes. New Testaments, almost unknown to the ordinary Russian, were distributed in tens of thousands from the Neva and the Vistula to prison camps in Siberia. Prayer meetings began in place after place.

But the wrath of the Russian Orthodox Church was roused. Government officials, terrified of anything which might undermine the autocracy, determined to suppress the Evangelical Revival. Alexander II, shortly before he was blown to pieces by a Nihilist bomb, reluctantly agreed to outlaw the movement in which his friend Paschkov was taking so large a part. Paschkov was banished. Count Korff, Lord Chamberlain, and a whole array of princesses and counts were ordered to their estates or forbidden the realm. Lesser men were sent in chains to Siberia. "I have been praying that God would use me among prisoners," cried one, "and now my prayer is answered."

"Radstockism," as its detractors called the movement, was sent underground. But if in England the Methodist Revival prevented revolution in 1789, it may well have been that the Evangelical Revival of the seventies, had it been allowed to take its course, would have so purified Russian life and government that the revolution of 1917, with all the misery that Communism has brought the world, would never have occurred. God gave Russia her opportunity, and His Wesley was Lord Radstock.

Excluded from Russia, Radstock's work was not done. In Sweden, Denmark, Finland, and often in Paris, now republican and bitter in defeat, he moved quietly among both upper classes and the poor. Seven times he went to India, and in 1897 he organized a scheme by which every native official received a New Testament on Queen Victoria's Jubilee.

At home, news of his work in Russia opened doors hitherto closed among the aristocracy of England; his ambition to reach his own class was rewarded, though without spectacular results. And scarcely an evangelical work or mission was untouched by him. For over thirty years, almost to the Great War, his name crosses and recrosses the story of England's religious movements. The Cambridge Seven* were influenced by him; he helped Moody and Sankey, and Torrey and Alexander; man after man on the mission field or in home service could point to some moment when an address or a personal word from Radstock changed the course of their lives.

The missionary to Imperial Russia died in December 1913, little more than three years before the Revolution. His name remains a reminder of the power of a life lived in constant communion with the Lord Jesus.

* See the next chapter for the story of the Cambridge Seven.

7. Stroke Oar

O_n a bluff April day in 1882 the river banks of the Thames were crowded once again from Putney to Mortlake to watch the annual Oxford-Cambridge boat race. Cambridge had the inside station and was away to a good start. But on the Umpire's launch, chugging slowly behind with a swarming trail of little boats, it was soon seen that the Cambridge Eight were not together. By Hammersmith, the Oxford Eight were level and excitement was intense. In a few moments they were ahead and, as Stanley Smith the Cambridge stroke ruefully remarked, "we were treated to their wash, after which we went awfully; and finally Oxford won by seven lengths!"

Though Oxford had won, the critics were loud in

their praise of the Cambridge stroke, who had given a splendid exhibition of oarsmanship. Three years later this popular young stroke oar with his "handsome address and winning manners" was a humble missionary in China. And the manner of his going made a stir across the world and lit fires still burning. The "Cambridge Seven" will never be forgotten.

The event which put S. P. Smith on the road to China was the visit of the American evangelist Moody to Cambridge University in November 1882. The mission began in derision and ended with "the most remarkable meeting ever seen in Cambridge," a University transformed, and proud undergraduates humbled at the foot of the Cross.

Smith had already finished Cambridge and was working as a schoolmaster in South London. But as a former member of the Cambridge Inter-Collegiate Christian Union, he took leave for the weekend, and was stirred to the depths by what he saw. "Marvellous," he wrote, "verily God's measure is *running over*." Smith had been a Christian since he was twelve. From a fluctuating introspective faith he had passed to settled determination to serve Christ. But it had been on his own terms, with much "insincerity, sham and 'men service.' " Never before had he seen God's unfettered power, nor realized his own insignificance.

Though humbled, Stanley Smith had more to learn before God could show him his life's work. The scene changes to a little seaside village on the east coast—Pakestone, Norfolk, on a raw January day two months later. Smith, staying with friends nearby, is spending a night as guest of an elderly, gentle Christian, Mr. Price. They have spoken together at an Old Folks' meeting and now are deep in talk. Through long experience Price had learned "the secret of liberty and delight in the service of the Lord"—an utter yeilding to Christ, "turning your life of duty into a life of liberty and love."

As they talked Smith realized that he did not possess the secret. The next day, in simple faith, he asked God to take his whole life and use it. Immediately his experience was transformed. "Bless the dear Lord," he could write a few days later, "He is in me and *fills* me. How good He is. Oh that all Christians knew this full surrender." Thenceforth his work, his athletics, his friendships became one unhesitant happy witness to Christ, and time was spent preaching, and bringing others to know Christ as Savior or, knowing Him, to yield to Him as Lord.

But if Smith thought he was now ready he was wrong. Clear command for the future was not given for ten months, until the last day of November 1883. At a country vicarage in Surrey, close to Leith Hill, Smith was a speaker at a weekend convention. During that weekend a verse of Scripture was so burned into his consciousness that he saw it as a call from his Lord demanding instant response: "I will give thee for a light to the Gentiles, that thou mayst be my salvation unto the end of the earth." For Smith it was a marching order for the mission field.

He offered himself to Hudson Taylor and the China Inland Mission, and in due course was accepted. Nor was that all. Smith felt an urge to awaken others to their responsibilities to the Christ-less millions overseas. Before long, after talks and prayer together, a Cambridge friend joined him— Willie Cassels, a London curate. Independently a gunner subaltern, D. E. Hoste, was being led the same road. Two brothers, sons of a wealthy Member of Parliament and both former members of the Eton cricket Eleven, one a Cambridge man converted through Moody, the other a cavalry officer won by his brother, were also sensing the call. Smith met them and encouraged them. One of his greatest Cambridge friends also joined. The climax came with C. T. Studd, the most brilliant all-round cricketer of the day, an Eton, Cambridge, and England player, who in November 1884, after going with Smith to a C.I.M. meeting, determined to leave all and follow Christ to the ends of the earth.

Thus was born the Cambridge Seven. In an age to which, in Britain, wealth and breeding meant as much as athletic distinction, the challenge of such a team was irresistible. Smith and Studd toured universities and cities in England and Scotland, setting alight a fire of revival. In three great meetings, at Cambridge, Oxford, and in London, the whole Seven told in simple terms how Christ had called them. The last meeting, in the Exeter Hall in the Strand on a pouring wet night in February 1885, was so crowded and enthusiastic that the report of it circled the world and led in time to the forming of the Student Missionary Volunteers, first in America and then in Great Britain.

From the Boat Race of '82 to China in '85 and the rise of a new missionary consciousness among students seemed far. But S. P. Smith was an ordinary person. What he learned others may learn, with consequences as far-reaching. Personal surrender and victory; patient waiting for the unmistakable call; prompt obedience; unfettered rejoicing in the privilege of proclaiming Christ at home and abroad; all this was component in the discovery of his vocation. And after that, for Stanley Smith, nearly fifty years of humble, enduring service in the dusty plains of China, with few and brief visits home, until his death at Tsechow in Shansi on January 31, 1931.

8. Cannibal Easter

A mob of *howling, naked,* war-painted savages swarmed around a native house above the sandy foreshore of a river mouth in unexplored New Guinea on an afternoon in December 1877. Inside the house a white woman sat sewing. The movement of her fingers gave no indication of her fervent but not quite agitated inward praying. Near her crouched three Polynesian teachers and their wives. Strong Christians from distant South Sea islands, they were struggling now with the uncomfortable conviction that their missionary service was about to end summarily in a cooking pot.

Down on the shore the white woman's husband had been signaling to his lugger for some stores when he heard the commotion behind. James Chalmers, a strongly built Scotsman of thirty-six with bushy black beard, ran up to the native house, pushed his way through a ring of cannibals, and climbed the platform.

"One evil-looking fellow wearing a human jawbone and carrying a heavy stone club rushed towards me as if to strike," Chalmers wrote later. "Looking him steadily in the face our eyes met, and I demanded in loud, angry tones what he wanted." By signs and unintelligible noises the cannibal demanded tomahawks, knives, iron and beads, "and that if they were not given they were going to kill us."

"You may kill us," shouted the white man, "but never a thing will you get from us." His tones conveyed the intensity of his displeasure to men whose language he had not yet had time to learn.

A Polynesian teacher approached. "Tamate," he implored the white man, using Chalmers' South Seas name and speaking in the language of Rarotonga, the island which they had all left to evangelize New Guinea, "please give him a little something or we will all be murdered!"

"No," Tamate replied. "Can't you see that if I give them something because they threaten us, every group in the district will try the same trick. When there's nothing left they will murder us. Let them murder us now and be done with it!"

One of the cannibals, a friendly man from the house where the missionaries had lived since their landing three days earlier, told Tamate by signs that the violent savages came from across the river. He had better give them something to get rid of them.

Tamate, ignoring the angry roars and brandished clubs, smiled at him but shook his head. He would not give anything to armed men. "We have never carried arms and have lived among you as friends." The friendly cannibal harangued the crowd—which then retired to consider the situation. Thus the immediate danger was past. A deputation came forward to repeat the request, and again met refusal. Then they dispersed.

Next day their chief came, unarmed and unpainted, to say "Sorry!" Tamate grinned happily at him, took him into the house and gave him a present. Jeanie Chalmers, still sewing, prayed that the cannibal would soon receive the Best Gift of all.

James and Jeanie Chalmers had served some ten years in the settled island of Rarotonga before pioneering in New Guinea. James Chalmers, "Tamate," was the son of a stonemason in the western highlands of Scotland, where he had been thoroughly grounded in the deep if stern religious convictions of an unbending Calvinism. He had even determined as a boy to be a missionary to cannibals, but subsequently decided that he was not among God's elect. Missionary ambition faded in favor of allowing full play to an irrepressible sense of fun. His practical jokes and youthful escapades sent shudders through the staid little fishing port of Inveraray, nestling beside the great castle of the Duke of Argyll.

When Chalmers was eighteen, during the revival of 1859, two evangelists were invited to Inveraray. Chalmers attended a meeting in a loft during a heavy rainstorm and there became aware of the truth of Christ, through the verse from Revelation, "Let him that is athirst come. And whosoever will, let him take the water of life freely."

During training in England he showed himself more than ever a leader—in student pranks as well as in evangelism. A young man of strength, high spirits, humor and intense dedication, he "used to pray for help as if he were at his mother's knee, and to preach as though he were sure of the message he had then to deliver."

His arrival on the mission field was, characteristically though unintentionally, unconventional. The ship was wrecked on a reef in Samoa, and James and Jeanie chartered the brig of a local white pirate whom Chalmers temporarily tamed!

"Tamate," as he was named by the South Sea islanders, had hoped to pioneer at once, but the leaders of the London Missionary Society kept him nearly ten years in an island already evangelized. At last, with a group of his own Rarotongans, he was allowed to adventure into New Guinea. Only six years earlier a small group of missionaries had become the earliest white settlers in a land where strangers lived in hourly expectation of being clubbed, cooked, and eaten. (A friendly native tried to present Jeanie with a portion of oven-fresh human breast.)

After that first landing, which had so nearly ended in death, Chalmers placed a chain of Polynesian teacher-evangelists along the southern coast of New Guinea (Papua). In each place he made the first, dangerous contact and stayed until the Papuans were reasonably friendly. He was a man whom they immediately respected and soon loved—tall, strong, impulsive, generous, quick-tempered but quick to laugh. He had no trace of a white man's pomposity, yet his character conveyed such authority that no native liked to cross him. He was fearless, again and again taking his life in his hands. And he brimmed over with a genuine, utterly unsentimental love, knowing that even the most depraved and cruel could be transformed by the love and Spirit of Christ.

Tamate's methods were always unconventional. He had no horror of using tobacco or tomahawks as currency. Once he caused merriment in the city of London by cabling: "Send one gross tomahawks, one gross butcher knives. Going east try make friends between tribes." He was a great explorer, but always as a means of spreading the gospel. He found a people sunk in degradation, violence and fear. Chalmers knew that his hard and dangerous labor was worthwhile because in time "all these evils would yield to the gospel. God is Love, seen in Christ: this was the life word we brought them. The gospel was working its way in bush-clearing, fencing, planting, housebuilding; through fun, play, feasting, travelling, joking, laughing, and along the ordinary experience of everyday life."

Tamate lived Christ. He preached Christ as the one who could save to the uttermost those who came to Him. And he rejoiced at last to hear a young Papuan, so recently a cannibal, say to his fellow tribesmen, "The time has come to be up and doing. Foreigners have brought us the gospel; many have died of fever, several have been speared and tomahawked. Now let us carry the gospel to other districts and if we die, it is well: we die in Christ. If we are murdered, it is well: it is in carrying His name and love, and will be for Him. Let us to it!"

For twenty-three years Tamate and his Polynesians and Papuans evangelized, pacified, and civilized great stretches of the New Guinea coastland, and up into the nearer mountains as far as they could go. While her husband pioneered, Jeanie stayed bravely in their first cannibal village in order to show the trust that always breeds trust, but eventually the climate drove her to Australia where she died. After nine lonely years Tamate married again. It was soon after this that Robert Louis Stevenson, then living in Polynesia, described him in letters home as "a man nobody can see and not love. . . . A big, stout, wildish-looking man, iron grey, with big bold black eyes and a deep furrow down each cheek. . . . With no humbug, plenty of courage, and the love of adventure. . . . He has plenty of faults like the rest of us but he's as big as a church."

All this time Tamate had no permanent white helper. "We need help," he wrote home, "missionaries willing to live among the savages, men and women who will joyfully endure the hardship of the climate for Christ's sake." When at length he heard that someone was appointed he commented, "I hope he is a good all-around man without namby-pambyism, ready for all sorts of roughing it." And in Oliver Tomkins he found a man after his heart.

Within weeks of Tomkins' arrival Chalmers' second wife fell ill. In the long period of nursing her before she died, the young recruit became as a dear son to the veteran. After the burial they spent months touring the settled stations which Tomkins would supervise. Then they set off for the notorious Aird River delta where Tamate planned to pioneer, along coasts which no missionary had penetrated, where Christ had "not been named." He had reconnoitered the area, knew "the savages there are splendid fellows. If only I can get hold of them they will make splendid missionaries."

As Tamate and Tomkins, with their party consisting of a Polynesian teacher, a Papuan Christian chief and ten embryo Papuan missionaries, approached Goaribari Island, it happened that the inhabitants of a village named Dopina had just completed a new *dubu* or communal house for fighting men. Built of sago-palm timber, a *dubu* was not ready for use without human sacrifice. The next strangers to the island would serve for the consecration and the feast.

When the mission lugger rounded the headland, the men of the village at once paddled out and swarmed aboard. Tamate was used to such invasions, the normal prelude to his entry into a new village.

It was Easter Sunday evening, April 7th, 1901. As the sun dropped swiftly to the brief tropical dusk, Tamate promised to visit the village in peace. He tried in vain to persuade the armed men to leave the vessel. To draw them off he said he would go ashore at once in the whale boat for half an hour and be back for supper. Tomkins said he would go too. They set off, crewed by the ten mission boys and the chief.

Tamate knew nothing about the new *dubu,* but he was ready as always "to die for the name of the Lord Jesus." Young Tomkins had no fear of death either.

The boat reached shore. While the chief and most of the mission boys stayed on guard, the two missionaries accepted the villagers' pressing invitation to enter the *dubu* for refreshment. They sat down on the floor, Tamate cracking jokes with his new neighbors and, as always, praying in his heart to the Companion whose Easter message he brought. All around him in the fading light were piles of human skulls at the feet of coarse wooden images.

Two swift blows from behind by stone clubs. Two cassowary-bone daggers swiftly plunged into the gullets of the white men. While the mission boys were set upon and murdered, the heads of Tamate and Tomkins were severed from their bodies. They were stripped, deftly cut into joints and passed to the women to be cooked, mixed with sago.

To the Western world, when the news came, the Easter massacre seemed a foul and obscene ending to two lives of goodwill—one famous and honored, one young and promising. To the people of the village the cannibal feast was the prelude to their eventual discovery of Christ.

To Tamate and Tomkins it was a painless transition from the Easter Faith to the Easter Presence.

9. Left in Lagos

Sitting at the back of a newly opened church in Toronto in the early eighteen-nineties, a young man heard the great missionary statesman, A. J. Gordon deliver his famous lectures on the Holy Spirit in Missions. Before the series ended the young listener, Rowland V. Bingham, was praying that the Spirit would call him to serve in some distant, lonely corner of the earth.

He went on with his obscure pastorate in the countryside near Toronto. The months passed without a clear answer to his prayer. Then he happened to address a small morning meeting in the city, where an elderly lady with a distinct Scottish accent invited him home for lunch, introducing herself as a Mrs. Gowans, a widow. During and after lunch she told him of her son Walter, who had been certain that he was called to take the gospel to the neediest country he could find. He had pored over maps and statistics until one vast area in Africa had impressed itself on him as almost totally without Christian witness.

From coast to coast, south of the Sahara and north of the rain forests lay a great, populated belt known in the nineties as the Sudan. Its eastern regions had been wrested by the fanatical Moslem Mahdi from the Anglo-Egyptian rule of General Gordon, murdered at Khartoum seven years before. The French were pushing into its northern-western area, the British were probing from the Gold Coast (Ghana) and up the Niger from Lagos, but almost all the land lay under the rule of slave-raiding Moslem kings or animist tribal chieftains. Before Rowland Bingham left Mrs. Gowans, he knew in his heart that he must join Walter Gowans to penetrate the Sudan with the message of the Lord Jesus.

On a fare scraped together by his farmer friends, and with a college contemporary of Gowans, Tom Kent, whom he met in New York, Bingham sailed to England where Gowans had gone ahead, since the mighty British Empire on which the sun never set was the colonial power in the region, and it was a British missionary board who must send them. But, like Hudson Taylor when he tried to persuade existing societies to evangelize inland China, Gowans, Bingham, and Kent met total refusal for inland Sudan: money was too short, they were told, and the climate was a killer.

The three young men decided to go ahead on their own; they had just enough money to reach Lagos and the Lord would provide from there. On December 4th, 1893, they were anchored off this fever-haunted port which had as yet no harbor for big ships. Missionaries of the three societies working on the coast befriended them to the extent of introducing a tough old trader who rented them a home and, rough sinner as he was, went far beyond the claims of business to help them. But as for going inland, the three North Americans were told they were mad.

Rowland Bingham fell ill with the dreaded malaria which carried off so many in the "White Man's Grave." There was no known cure at that date, and at sunset the doctor sent a message to the Anglican mission home: he could not last the night. None of the Americans was Episcopalian but the newly arrived bishop, a burly New Zealander named Joseph Hill, came across to pray with Bingham, then gathered the missionaries to special prayer on his behalf. "Do you believe," he asked one of them as they rose from their knees, "that we are going to receive that for which we have asked?"

"I do!" she replied. "I believe that young man is going to be raised up." And he was; but less than a week later Bishop Hill and his wife were both dead of yellow fever, he in the afternoon and she at midnight; of all the party of ten he had brought out only one survived.

When Bingham was strong enough to work again, he and his companions resolved that it was high time to leave for the far interior, for the central Sudan which, Gowan said, was closed only because no one would open the door. They sold almost all their belongings, including their watches, yet still had not enough to pay porters and boatmen—until the mail steamer arrived carrying a gift of $500 from a servant girl called Mary Jones: she had been left a legacy and sent it all to this new, untried, unnamed mission, together with a smaller amount which her mistress added.

By now Gowans, Kent, and Bingham had realized that one of them must be left in Lagos to arrange for the despatch up country of further supplies, for they had no field secretary or committee: the Lagos missionaries, in the kindest possible way, had washed their hands of them, yet they could not live in the interior without trade goods with which to barter, for money was unknown. Unless they engaged porters to carry rolls of calico and sacks of beads, knives, and other odds and ends highly regarded by the tribes, they would be reduced to beggary. Until they could establish a mission station, grow crops and breed cattle, they must depend on more trade goods sent from the coast.

Raymond Bingham, as the convalescent, was the obvious choice to remain behind, however disappointed he might be that he would as yet only see the Sudan interior by the eye of faith and prayer. Gowans and Kent waved good-by and disappeared up the Niger River, beyond the invisible line which marked the frontier of Lagos Colony, into the distant north. They could not know that they were several years too early: both the pacification, which created

Nigeria and ended the tyranny of slave-raiding emirs, and the momentous discovery of the cause of malaria lay only a little in the future, but that little meant death.

Gowans and Kent reached a town about six hundred miles from Lagos. Its chief, a fetish worshiper, welcomed them partly because he hoped for a white man's protection from the powerful Moslem emirs whose armies ranged at will. Gowans decided to settle and begin preaching, using his newly acquired, little-tried facility in Hausa, the language most widely used in West Africa. Tom Kent set off to bring up further supplies of trade goods from the coast.

He had not been gone many days when the war drums sounded, the women and children ran screaming into the square and the men rounded up their stunted cattle and drove them behind the walls of thorn and timber. A Moslem emir was approaching on a slave raid. For two weeks Gowans lived the life of the besieged, his health rapidly worsening, until the town fell to assault while the thatched circular huts went up in flames. The emir enslaved the survivors and drove off their cattle. He offered elegant courtesies to the white man but appropriated his trade goods, cannily offering slaves in payment knowing they would be refused.

Gowans, expelled, reduced to penury, desperately weak, died of malaria on the way back to the coast.

Kent was ignorant of this tragedy when he reached Lagos after an appalling journey. Bingham nursed him back to health, and accompanied him as far inland as he could go while maintaining their contact with Lagos. Tom Kent went forward to rejoin Gowans—and did so literally, for he too died of malaria, a year and four days after the three young men had landed.

In 1895 Raymond Bingham, the last of the three, returned to North America to find reinforcement and to put the "Sudan Interior Mission," as it was eventually named, on a secure footing. He did not manage to advance on the Sudan again for five years, but in that time he had gained further experience in pastorate and hospital, had won a wife, formed a Mission Council—with flimsy enough finance—and sailed joyfully in 1900 with two other young men.

They landed; the Lagos missionaries were as adamant as before that this was a fool's errand. And when Bingham once more, within three weeks, developed malaria and was told it was a choice of death in Lagos or survival by going back on the steamer which had brought him, they seemed proved right. "It would have been easier for me, perhaps," wrote Bingham in his autobiography, "had I died in Africa, for on that homeward journey I died another death. Everything seemed to have failed, and when, while I was gradually regaining strength in Britain, a fateful cable reached me with word that my two companions were arriving shortly, I went through the darkest period of my life."

The two companions had been persuaded to give up by the Lagos missionaries—and disappeared into oblivion.

Thus, seven years after Bingham had set out with such sure hopes from Mrs. Gowans' parlor, his mission was a mere mockery. But Mrs. Gowans' response to her son's death had been: "I would rather have had Walter go out to the Sudan and die there all alone, than have him home, disobeying his Lord." And Raymond Bingham, too, determined to continue to obey, whether it led to ridicule or death.

Most of his Council urged the disbanding of this Sudan Interior Mission that never was. One member backed Bingham. And four more young men offered. This time he sent them to healthier parts to learn the language before they all went to Lagos. Furthermore, he had met Frederick Lugard who had recently defeated the slaver emirs and was on his way back to the central Sudan to form the peaceful protectorate of Nigeria. Lord Lugard, as he became, admired young Bingham and did all he could to encourage the missionaries. On his advice they made their first home away from the river valleys to avoid the mosquito for the short time remaining before quinine stopped malaria being a fatal disease.

The next seven years saw a growing Mission, one or two deaths—and no conversions whatever. But when Bingham died in 1943, the international, interdenominational Sudan Interior Mission was already numerically one of the largest, with strong national churches growing around it. Today, right across from West Africa to Ethiopia, despite past persecutions and the difficulties inevitable in a rapidly changing world, these churches represent a powerful witness to Jesus Christ, their national pastors teamed with Western missionaries like a mighty army. The printing press Bingham founded pours out Christian literature. The voice of Radio Station ELWA carries the message from coast to coast.

All, under God, because one man, left in Lagos, refused to abandon his call.

10. Santa Claus of the North

One Christmas morning in the early nineteen hundreds the people of a small isolated fishing village in Labrador were gathered outside their doors watching an unusual sight. A sledge was coming towards them across the frozen bay. But instead of the team of husky dogs it was drawn by a reindeer—an animal unknown in Labrador, though closely related to the wild caribou of the forests. The sledge drew nearer and the fishermen and their wives—descendants of the original British settlers—soon saw that the sledge carried their great friend, the Good Samaritan of the Coast, Wilfred Grenfell.

Crowding round him as he unloaded his surgical instruments for an emergency operation, they asked him how and why he had put a stag into harness. "Milk! Milk! Milk!" he replied, at which they blinked, though they knew the doctor's jovial ways. After a little more leg-pulling, he explained that he had introduced a herd of domestic reindeer from Lapland as a substitute for dairy cows, which could not exist on the Coast, thus hoping to provide people with the fresh milk they sorely needed. Some of the stags he was using for transport. Marveling at the doctor's unending ideas for their assistance, the rugged fisherfolk waited while he performed the surgery for which he had come, and then joined him for a simple Christmas service, lustily singing the old hymns and listening with bowed heads as Grenfell prayed extempore in the most natural, unaffected manner.

Grenfell had already done much to transform the lives of the scattered fishing and trapping communities of Labrador. In the snowy wastes of the North he was a veritable embodiment of the Christmas spirit, bringing throughout the year good things for body and soul alike. To him this was no matter for boasting, but just a response to one of his favorite verses from the Psalms, "Teach me to do the thing that pleaseth Thee."

It all traced back to a winter's day in the slums of East London early in 1885. Grenfell, a young medical student in his second year, a keen rowing man and rugby football player and devoted to the sea and outdoor life, happened to wander into a large tent erected on a piece of derelict ground in dockland, near where he had been sent to attend a case. He found himself in a meeting of Moody and Sankey's second London campaign. "It was so new to me," records Grenfell, "that when a tedious prayer bore began with a long oration, I started to leave. Suddenly the leader, who I learned afterwards was D. L. Moody, called out to the audience, 'Let us sing a hymn while our brother finishes his prayer.' His practicality interested me and I stayed the service out." He left "with a determination either to make religion a real effort to do as I thought Christ would do in my place as a doctor, or frankly abandon it."

For some weeks he hovered; to come out for Christ in the "coarse and evil environment" of the hospital medical school required more pluck than even Wilfred Grenfell possessed. Then he attended a meeting at which the speakers were the Studd brothers—it was a short while before C. T. Studd sailed with the Cambridge Seven. The fact that they were noted athletes made Grenfell hang on their words. "I felt I could listen to them. I could not have listened to a sensuous-looking man, a man who was not a master of his own body." At the end of the service the Studds asked all those who would give their lives to Christ to stand up. There was dead silence and no one stirred. "It seemed a very sensible question to me," wrote Grenfell, "but I was amazed how hard I found it to stand up. At last one boy, out of a hundred or more in sailor rig from a reformatory ship on the Thames, suddenly rose. It seemed to me such a wonderfully courageous act—for I knew perfectly what it would mean to him—that I immediately found myself on my feet."

Grenfell scorned mere theorizing. He had no truck with people who talked pious and never lifted a finger to serve Christ or their fellows. At once he began work among the boys in his neighborhood, running a Sunday school with such vigor that the staid parson, shocked by his introduction of boxing on weekday evenings, forced him to resign. He therefore joined up with a "ragged school," which with East End boys in the eighties required as much physical hardihood as spiritual zeal. To this he added lodging-house work and temperance campaigning in the worst of the slum saloons. Once the angry topers made preparations to beat him up and pour whiskey down his throat: "however they greatly overrated their stock of fitness and equally underrated my good training, for the scrimmage went all my way in a very short time."

Grenfell's holidays were always spent sailing, with his brother and a few friends hiring an old fishing smack in the Irish sea. "One result of these holidays was that I told my London boys about them, using one's experiences as illustrations, till suddenly it struck me that this was shabby Christianity." After that, he always took some of them with him, and in subsequent summers he ran camping and boating holidays on the Welsh coast, with straight-from-the-shoulder talks on the Christian life to end each day.

From sailing holidays to service on the sea was a natural move. Shortly after he had qualified as a doctor and finished his hospital training, his great friend and teacher, the brilliant surgeon Sir Frederick Treves, told him that a recently formed mission (afterwards the Royal National Mission to Deep Sea Fishermen) was looking for a doctor to help them among the North Sea herring fleet which stayed at sea for months at a time. They had "chartered a small fishing smack, and sent her out among the fishermen to hold religious services of a simple, unconventional type, in order to afford the men an alternative to the grog vessels when fishing was slack." Grenfell joined at Yarmouth, wondering whether he would be of any use among such men "far older and tougher and more experienced than I." But on the wheel of the Mission ship was engraved "Follow Me and I will make you fishers of men." "That was a real challenge," recalled Grenfell, "and I knew then perfectly well that that was my only chance, anyhow."

Four years later, in 1892, he set out at the Mission's invitation to cross the far north of the Atlantic in a sailing vessel to see if he could help the fishermen of Labrador and North Newfoundland. The coasts would be wild, lonely and cold, though the expedition was only for the few summer months. But the venture seemed no sacrifice to Grenfell. "I have always believed that the Good Samaritan went across the road to the wounded man just because he wanted to," he once remarked. And besides, there was "everything about such a venture as sailing to Labrador to attract my type of mind."

After calling at St. Johns they made landfall in Labrador. "A serried rank of range upon range of hills, reaching north and south as far as the eye could see from the masthead, was rising above our

93

horizon behind a very surfeit of islands." At their
first harbor they were bombarded with calls for medical help from ships and shore. That evening, when
the last patient had left the spotless dispensary on
board the mission schooner, Grenfell noticed "a miserable bunch of boards, serving as a boat, with only
a dab of tar along its seams lying motionless a little
way from us. In it, sitting silent, was a half-clad,
brown haired, brown faced figure." After a prolonged
stare the man in the boat suddenly said "Be you a
doctor?" "That's what I call myself," replied Grenfell with the twinkle in his eyes which was to become
so well known and loved throughout Labrador. "Us
hasn't got no money," said the half-clothed settler,
"but there's a very sick man is here, if so be you'd
come and see him."

Grenfell was led to a small, bare, filthy hovel,
crowded with neglected children. "A very sick man
was coughing his soul out in the darkness while a
pitiably covered woman gave him cold water to sip
out of a spoon." The man's case was hopeless and
with his death starvation would be a grim reality for
the whole family; government relief was a mockery
because of the iniquities of the local trading system.
Thus Grenfell was faced with something of the need
of Labrador. As he put it, "to pray for the man, and
with the family was easy, but scarcely satisfying."
Grenfell knew that Christ would not have him leave
it at that.

And thus year by year he returned to Labrador, to
do what he could for their bodies and souls, and at
last made his home on the Coast and stayed the

whole year round. Among the bleak headlands and scattered islands washed by roaring seas in summer and gripped by ice in winter, wherever ship or sledge could take him, he carried the love of Christ, not in word only but in deeds. His frank speech laced with the merry yarns that the fisherfolk loved brought him right to their hearts. And they knew that he was as skillful and hardy a sailor as themselves.

He soon found that much of the misery of the Coast was caused by the grip of corrupt traders, aided by an outdated system of commerce. He proposed the creation of cooperative stores. The vested interests of the colony were enraged and made common cause to crush him. Moreover the settlers who stood to gain most were afraid to join and when he persuaded them, "not one shareholder wished to have his name registered, and one and all they were opposed to having the little building labelled as a store—so ingrained was their fear of their suppliers." But despite setbacks and losses, Grenfell's scheme survived, and like the hospitals and dispensaries and schools which he built, helped to make the life of the settlers more tolerable and to open their hearts to the gospel.

On one voyage his little hospital ship had dropped anchor among a group of islands. "Suddenly a boat bumped our side and a woman climbed over the rail with a bundle under each arm. On my chartroom table she laid the two bundles and proceeded to untie them." They proved to be twin babies, "blind as kittens." The mother had four other children and her husband had been killed in an accident three months earlier. "What ever are you going to do with the babies?" asked Grenfell. "Give them to you, Doctor."

When the ship was under way again, in a choppy sea, the babies howled so loudly that the helmsman "stuck his head into the chartroom, which was directly behind the wheelhouse." "What are you going to do with those, sir?" he asked. "Shh," replied Grenfell, "they're blind and quite useless. When we get outside, we'll drop them over the rail." "He stared at me for a second," records Grenfell, "before he turned back to the wheel. A few minutes later in popped his head again. 'Excuse my being so bold, but don't throw them over the side. We've got eight of our own, but I guess my wife'll find a place for those two.'" Grenfell laughingly told him that he had already begun to form a collection of derelict children at his base at St. Anthony's, to which these would be added.

And thus the work grew. As the years passed, Grenfell's fame spread across North America and in Britain, and funds and volunteers flowed to his aid. After the First World War, in an age which tended to divorce social welfare from spirituality and in which many of the younger generation were ashamed of open profession of faith, Grenfell stood as a virile example of practical Christian love which counts service a privilege and spices it with humor and a refusal to be beaten. "The King Himself," he once wrote, "cannot win His battle without us, He having entrusted us with the task, ensuring victory if we 'are bound to Him.'"

Grenfell was often near death as he made his way

through ice and storms on sea and land. At Easter 1908, at the age of forty-three, he was caught with his team of huskies on a pan of ice during a sudden thaw and was rapidly drifting out to sea, to drown, or die by cold and starvation if the ice-pan held out. "My own faith in the mystery of immortality is so untroubled that it now seemed almost natural to be passing the portal of death from an ice-pan. Quite unbidden the words of the old hymn kept running through my head, 'Oh, help me from my heart to say, Thy will be done.'"

He was rescued just in time. A full span of life was given him, for the good of Labrador and the glory of Christ; and he died in 1940 at the age of seventy-five, after only five years retirement away from his beloved Coast.

11. Victims of the Long March

*I*t was a prosaic, peaceful world, though locally there had been disturbances from bandits and Communists. America was immersed in the New Deal, England with preparations for the Silver Jubilee of King George V. Hitler was not yet a menace and the League of Nations still had respect. War, bloodshed and murder were not much in mind, and as for new names on the roll of Christian martyrs, the possibility, in October 1934, seemed so remote as to be almost absurd.

A young American and a middle-aged Englishman were closeted with the district magistrate of Tsingteh, Anhwei, a decayed little town a few hundred miles from Nanking. The American and the Englishman were missionaries of the China Inland Mission.

Martyrdom was far from the thoughts of John Stam, the young American, as he listened to his senior colleague asking the magistrate whether it would be safe for John to bring his wife and their month-old baby to live in Tsingteh. The magistrate admitted that there had been banditry, for the countryside was half-starving, but was soothing in his protestations of security.

John Stam remarked that they did not want to meet the Communists, who had been passing through the next province during their famous "long march" after defeat in South China.

"Oh, no, no!" the magistrate exclaimed. "There is no danger of Communists here. As far as that is concerned you may come at once and bring your family. I will guarantee your safety, and if there should be any trouble you can come to my *yamen*."

A month later John and Betty Stam and the baby, Helen Priscilla, made their home in the disused Tsingteh mission compound in the middle of the town, with a background of distant mountains.

John Stam was twenty-eight, a tall athletic New Yorker whose Dutch extraction showed in his fair hair and blue eyes. Betty, a year younger, had been born in China, daughter of an American missionary doctor. They had met at Moody Bible Institute in Chicago. Both were unusual personalities. Betty, for instance, could write verse of distinction. And John, in Chicago, had deliberately tested his faith, like the .young Hudson Taylor at Hull eighty years earlier, by concealing his financial needs from his family and friends and depending only on God in prayer.

Betty had served her first year in China before John reached Shanghai. On October 25, 1933, a year to the day before the meeting with the magistrate, they had been married at Betty's home in North China. Two happy, unpretentious missionaries at the start of a lifetime of service, they were unreservedly dedicated to their call but aware of how much they had to learn, ready for the hardships and setbacks of Christian work in a foreign land, yet young enough to extract enjoyment from any situation. Their aim was simple: to "talk about Him to everybody, and live so closely with Him and in Him, that others may see that there really is such a person as Jesus."

Tsingteh was their first station on their own away from seniors. The opening ten days were much like any other missionary's introduction to a new location in China, with inquisitive Chinese crowding around so that privacy was impossible. The Stams visited the few Christians, preached in the little chapel, administered famine relief, and spoke on the streets to the chattering, restless press of peasants, soldiers, and townsfolk.

Early on the eleventh morning, December 6, 1934, Betty Stam was bathing the baby when a man ran in at the door. Out of breath and urging them to hurry, he panted that the magistrate had sent him to warn that the Communists, whom everybody had thought to be beyond the mountains, were advancing on the city after a surprise flank march behind the government army.

John at once sent for coolies and chairs, intending to join the stream of refugees who were hurrying down the street to escape to the safety of the hills. Before the Stams had put together their few necessities, a distant burst of firing proved that the battle had reached the town, where the Communists quickly scaled the walls and opened the gates. As the chair-coolies loped into the courtyard the Stams heard that the magistrate had fled. They bolted the door, realizing that escape was now impossible. Scattered shots, the crackle of flames, and the screams of townsfolk in the street made this all too obvious.

John told the servants to kneel. He began to lead in prayer, but the prayer was interrupted by a thundering knock on the door. Red soldiers demanded admittance. John spoke to them courteously. Betty, as calm as if the soldiers were inquirers for the faith, offered them tea and cakes. These were brusquely refused. John was tightly bound and taken across to the Communist headquarters. Betty and the baby were brought in later.

John and Betty stood together, bound, yet serene despite the suddenness of the catastrophe. The Stams had been allowed none of the mental or spiritual preparation which would have been theirs had these events occurred thirty years earlier, when the martyrdoms of the Boxer Rising were fresh in memory; or thirty years later, when the witness of Paul Carlson and the Congo martyrs rang round the world. The Stams faced death unwarned but their captors saw no trace of fear.

The Communists discussed the Americans' fate in their hearing. They were imperialists and should be liquidated. Moreover, the Communists detested

Christians. To make an example of two Christian leaders should strike terror into the hearts of the rest. The Reds had no compunction about murdering Americans, for the affair would merely increase the embarrassment of Chiang Kai-shek's government in Nanking.

The one difficulty was what to do with the baby. Betty heard them say that it had best be spitted on a bayonet in front of its parents.

A bystander, an old farmer, protested: "The baby has done nothing worthy of death!"

"Then it's your life for hers!" said the Red leader.

The Stams had never seen him before, and certainly had no claim on him, but their serenity and courage had gripped him. "I am willing," he said.

A moment later the man's severed head rolled across the floor.

The Communists abandoned Tsingteh, sacked and burning, and marched their prisoners to a town named Miaosheo. The looting and terror resumed while the Stams were left under guard in the postmaster's shop. The Stams had lived in Miaosheo and the postmaster knew them by sight.

"Where are you going?" he asked.

"We do not know where *they* are going," replied John, "but we are going to heaven."

That night the Stams were locked with their guards in an inner room of a deserted mansion. John was tied to a bedpost, but Betty was left free with the baby.

Next morning they were ordered to leave the baby and to strip off their outer garments and shoes—

though John managed to give Betty his socks. Then they were both bound tightly and led down the street while the Communists yelled ridicule and shouted to the townsfolk, many of whom had heard the Stams preach here in happier days, to come and see these Christians die. On a little hill outside the town they came to a clump of pines. A Communist began to harangue the trembling crowd, pouring scorn and blasphemies on all that the Stams held dear.

He was in full tilt when a man stepped boldly forward.

The Stams recognized him as Mr. Chang the medicine-seller, a nominal Christian who was known as "rather unwilling to witness for the true and living God." This once weak disciple fell on his knees and boldly pleaded for their lives. The Communists pushed him away. He persisted.

"Are you a Christian then?" they said.

Chang knew what his fate could be. "Yes," he replied.

He was dragged away to be butchered, and now it was John Stam's turn to intercede, for Chang. For reply John was ordered to kneel. People in that crowd said afterwards there was a "look of joy on his face."

The Chinese executioner, in time-honored style, held the sword level with both hands, whirled round and round to gather momentum, and struck. Betty was seen to quiver for a moment, then she fell unconscious across the body. A few moments later her head too was on the ground and the Reds were driving the crowd away.

Two days afterwards, when the Communists had left to spread their trail of bloodshed and fire further across the province, an evangelist of Miaosheo named Lo, whose leadership hitherto had been indifferent, returned with other refugees. Lo had heard rumors of the murder but found difficulty in obtaining facts because no one dared side with the Christians for fear lest the Reds return.

Following clues, he discovered the Stam baby, hungry but warm and alive in her zip-fastened sleeping bag in an abandoned house. He left her in the care of his wife.

Next he climbed the hillside where the headless bodies still lay, stiff and grotesque. He went back to the town and brought coffins, followed now by a crowd made braver through his courage. Lo and two other Christians, a woman and her son, placed the bodies in the coffins and bowed their heads in prayer. This formerly unsatisfactory half-hearted evangelist then turned to the crowd and told them that the Stams lived "in the presence of their heavenly Father. They came to China and to Miaosheo, not for themselves but for you, to tell you about the great love of God that you might believe in the Lord Jesus and be eternally saved. You have heard their message. Remember it is true. Their death proves it so. Do not forget what they told you—repent, and believe the gospel."

Many of the crowd were weeping as Lo set out on a

hundred-mile escape through the Communist-held territory, with his wife, to bring little Helen Stam to the nearest missionaries.

In the years that followed, many millions of men and women were to die by violence. But John and Betty were martyred in time of peace when such an event seemed incredible, and they died because of their faith. As always, the blood of martyrs was the seed of the church. The shock of their death turned timid Evangelist Lo into a courageous preacher. The story of their steadfastness prepared their fellow missionaries in China for the testing times of the Sino-Japanese and Pacific wars.

The impact on the student world was enormous, for the Stams had been fresh from college. One of those who gave herself for missionary service as a direct result of reading about the Stams was an American girl who became Mrs. Hector McMillan. Thirty years later she escaped death by inches in the Congo a few moments before her husband became one of the Stanleyville martyrs. As Ione McMillan had pledged herself to fill the gap in the missionary ranks left by the Stams, so her son, young Kenneth McMillan, as he lay wounded near the body of his father, pledged himself to return as a missionary to speak of Christ's love to the murderers.

12. Tuan Change

On the Sarawak coast in East Malaysia a missionary tapped excitedly at the typewriter as she compiled an information sheet datelined 1968: "Reports have been coming through of a great stirring among the churches of Indonesian Borneo. . . . Several Christians have had visions from the Lord which they have been told to proclaim to their people and as a result hundreds have repented from sin and turned to the Lord. The spiritual stirring is influencing Murut and Kelabit churches on the Sarawak border."

She glanced across the airstrip to the Bible School. They were just clearing up after the half yearly conference which 200 indigenous pastors and leaders had attended. Some had walked eight days through the jungle, others had come by mission plane or river boat, and they represented an expanding, missionary-hearted church of many tribes in the mountains and jungles of former British Borneo.

It all went back to the pioneering of one forgotten North American, William Ernest Presswood who, because he died young a few months after the end of World War II and lies buried in Borneo, has been largely forgotten except by those who loved him. But his name is legendary among the natives of the interior: they call him Tuan Change—because so many were changed from a particularly evil darkness into the light of Christ.

Ernie Presswood was born in the prairies of Canada in 1908, son of English immigrants. In a Sunday school class which could boast of eleven who later were ministers or missionaries, he gave his heart to Christ, yet it was not until the Presswoods returned to England briefly in the early 1920s, and he heard Gypsy Smith, that he dedicated himself for service. His father next bought a meat and grocery store in Toronto where Ernie trained as a motor mechanic. Then, after Prairie Bible School and the missionary institute at Nyack, N.Y., he joined the Christian and Missionary Alliance in the Netherlands East Indies during 1930.

About eighteen months later a most extraordinary rumor passed around the Murut or Dayak natives far upcountry in the interior. As it was told to me in Borneo long after, from a Murut named Panai Raub, "We were clearing the undergrowth for the new season's farming when we heard of a wonderful white man they called Tuan Change because he changed wicked natives and said they could have a new life. He was on an island off the coast." They wanted to go down but were afraid of venturing where Malays, Chinese, and whites lived.

The Muruts, a large tribe scattered across the mountains of the British-Dutch border, were steeped in spirit-worship to such an extent that planting would be endlessly delayed for lack of an omen, or the half-growing paddy abandoned at another. They turned most of the harvest into intoxicating rice-beer, sapped their tribal stamina by sexual malpractices, and frequently went head-hunting. They lived naked except for loin-cloths.

"When I heard," Panai Raub continued, " 'way up in the hills in the midst of all that drinking and fear of the spirits, about change and new life I just could not sleep for desire. Two months later when we were felling the big timber we heard that Tuan Change was downstream. We all went to meet him, taking our sick."

They found Presswood at Long Berang, a place above fearsome rapids which had needed considerable courage for a lone Westerner to negotiate, even with skilled boatmen. A huge crowd of Muruts, heads bowed, squatted round Presswood who was standing with eyes closed, arms outstretched to the sky.

"What is this?" thought Panai Raub, "What are they doing?"

After praying, Tuan Change unfolded some pictures, and preached in Malay with one of the few educated Muruts to interpret. Panai Raub was right in front.

"I could hear every word. Some of the others could not. He preached on the Resurrection, with amazing effect on the crowd. Right from the beginning it hit me. I was just drinking it in. When I first heard the Word I believed."

This was in September 1932. Next day Tuan Change left them and walked far over rugged jungle trails in great heat until forced back to the coast with a foot ulcerated by leech bites. He wrote home: "What a time I have had. Physically it has been a hard one but the results have been *glorious*. I think around 600 Dayaks were reached with the message."

Ernie Presswood was now nearly twenty-five. He was a true pioneer, willing to forgo the good things he enjoyed. He pushed himself relentlessly. "His middle name could have been 'hurry,' " writes one who knew him well. "It was always praying, reading, teaching, counseling, studying, and the little notebook always at hand." He seemed austere, not quick to laugh though with a genuine sense of humor. He was a perfectionist and could be hard on those who had openly acknowledged Christ yet failed Him, when Presswood would hide the compassion which ran strong within. His was a character that could be appreciated and admired by Muruts, who seemed so feckless then, yet subsequently disclosed the same characteristics of uncompromising dedication.

Presswood was kept at the coast by his bad foot until 1934 when he paid a second visit to Long Berang. "I have been here two weeks, twice as long as I expected, the interest has been so great. From early morning till late at night I have been kept busy with scarcely a break. Pray much for me for the strain is very great. Thus far I have baptized 130, and I expect there will be at least twice as many more." After a third, longer visit he returned to America, married Laura Harmon from Pennsylvania and in May 1937 they settled in Long Berang, having taken twenty-nine days negotiating the rapids.

That Christmas there was a great baptism at Long Berang; one of those baptized was Panai Raub. The following April, Presswood could write of a "morning service at which the Spirit of God was manifest in a very real way. Waves of praise swept over us as we looked into the faces of these happy Christians."

A few days later, when the Presswoods were still the only whites upriver, Laura had a miscarriage. Complications developed. There was nothing Ernie could do but see her die, and bury her in a coffin made with his own hands from one of the timbers with which they were building their home. Despite sorrowing natives he felt desperately alone. "Only those who have passed through such a heart-breaking experience can appreciate the distress." Then floods swept down on Long Berang, carrying away much of their precious timber. "Surely the Lord doesn't love me when He treats me thus, I thought: but He answered me so blessedly, 'Whom the Lord loveth He chasteneth and scourgeth every son He receives. . . .' The comfort and blessing that He has already sent upon my soul has strengthened me and given me courage to face the future."

For Borneo, it was already proving a great future, for the revival was spreading right across the border. The Sarawak Muruts had been even worse than the Indonesian. Officials of Rajah Brooke, the English ruler, estimated the whole community except the dogs to be drunk a hundred days in a year. After Tuan Change's first visit to Long Berang rumors of his good words had filtered over the border and some Sarawak Muruts went to find an Australian missionary, Hudson Southwell, who returned with them in 1933. Several were converted, but Rajah Brooke reckoned the Muruts were irredeemable. He refused Southwell permission to settle, threw a *cordon sanitaire* round the whole tribe, and left it to die out.

Panai Raub and other baptized Muruts determined to evangelize their cousins. Presswood had not told them they should. He so preached Christ that converts caught the vision for themselves; long before it became accepted missionary strategy Presswood urged that a church should be self-propagating and self-supporting.

"The first village I came to," Panai Raub says, "just over the border, a big drinking party was on. I refused it: 'I do not drink now.' 'Why not?' 'Because I follow the Lord Jesus Christ.' 'Where did you hear about Him?' 'From Tuan Change.' 'Does he live near this Lord Jesus?' They were very pleased and keen to hear. Even the old people who had been heavily involved in headhunting and the old worship brought the fetishes and burned them."

Panai Raub was not yet literate and no Scriptures had been translated; he preached with the aid of pictures. On his next visit he found that drinking had been abandoned. Wherever he went "there was not one house among the Muruts which did not want to hear. . . . 'Eternal life. *That's* what we want,' they would say." After he left, a village would choose its own church leaders from those who showed the gifts of the Spirit.

Late in 1938 the Rajah of Sarawak heard that something extraordinary had occurred. He ordered an expedition of inquiry, led by a government official and a missionary, who traveled among the Muruts from December 12, 1938 to February 4, 1939. The Government official reported that he was not popular with the Muruts because he smoked, drank whiskey, and did not possess a Sankey hymnbook! After that missionaries of the Borneo Evangelical Mission were allowed to settle.

Meanwhile across the border, Presswood undertook even more rigorous climbs to reach mountain villages, and by the time he left for his second furlough late in 1939 the Murut church was growing rapidly.

In America he was married again, to Ruth Brooks of Buffalo, N.Y., who returned with him in May 1940. He was appointed to head the Bible School at Makassar in the Celebes where the Japanese invasion engulfed him. Beaten, starved, forced to do coolie labor, kept in a pig house, he watched his brother missionaries die; even when giving a funeral address in a prison camp he was able to win men to Christ.

On November 27, 1945 the Presswoods returned to Borneo. Ernie discovered the grave of his successor, who had been bayoneted to death after surrendering to prevent reprisals on the natives. When the Presswoods went upcountry, they found that the war had divided loyalties, caused disputes and much backsliding, even some rebuilding of spirit-altars. "Such things were disheartening to Ernie," writes Ruth. But there were repentances, and much hunger.

Nor need Presswood have feared. The horrors of the Pacific War, the disturbances of the War of Independence and the checkered growth of Sukarno's Indonesia could not quench so deep a movement of the Spirit. Over the Sarawak border a great forward movement began in the 1950s, with the Muruts as the spearhead bringing the gospel to other tribes, while the Borneo Evangelical missionaries translated the Scriptures into the different languages, ran a Bible School, and set up their own air service.

Ernie Presswood did not live to see it. At Long Berang on that first post-war visit of January 1946, a severe bout of sickness convinced him, physically weak from his sufferings as a prisoner, that he must return downstream at once to the coast, several days early, or die. The river was high but a legend among the Muruts that natives tried to stop him traveling is disproved by contemporary letters. On Ernie's thirty-eighth birthday the Presswoods set off, with seven boatmen and another passenger carrying a live pig to sell at the market.

At the first rapid they had to land and crawl among the leeches through the edge of the undergrowth. After that the going was easier. "We continued shooting rapids for several hours and I found it fun," writes Ruth. At the last and biggest, the boatmen climbed up the mountain side to reconnoitre and reported it safe to negotiate, so they floated out past a big boulder. They were struck by a ten foot wave. The next capsized them. Ruth could not swim and Ernie grabbed her. They were carried downstream three hundred yards, much of it underwater.

They scrambled ashore, safe except for the baggage which was nearly all lost, and finally reached the coast after a trying journey in an overloaded motor boat wedged among prisoners of war.

The drenching seriously affected Presswood's shattered constitution. But he had promised to attend a conference across the bay, and though feeling ill, and Ruth sick and unable to accompany him, he kept his word. Pneumonia set in and on February 1, 1946 he died. His memorial is the vigorous evangelical church in Borneo.